D0547922

Managed Trade

The Case against Import Targets

Douglas A. Irwin

The AEI Press

Publisher for the American Enterprise Institute
WASHINGTON, D.C.

1994

Library of Congress Cataloging-in-Publication Data

Irwin, Douglas A., 1962–
    Managed trade : the case against import targets /
Douglas A. Irwin.
        p.   cm.
    Includes bibliographical references.
    ISBN 0-8447-3878-6. — ISBN 0-8447-3879-4 (pbk.)
        1. Import quotas—United States.   2. Imports—
Government policy—United States.   I. Title.
HF1455.I69   1994
382'.52'0973—dc20   94-19846
                                                                CIP

The AEI Press
Publisher for the American Enterprise Institute
1150 17th Street, N.W., Washington, D.C. 20036

Printed in the United States of America

Contents

iii

Acknowledgments

I wish to thank Claude Barfield, Michael Finger, Patrick Low, and especially Jagdish Bhagwati for helpful comments and criticisms. I also thank Lisa Mackey for superb research and graphics assistance.

The American Enterprise Institute would like to thank the Sasakawa Peace Foundation and the American Express Foundation for their support of this project.

ONE

Introduction

Voluntary import expansions are poised to become the latest weapon in the arsenal of U.S. trade policies to "open" foreign markets that are considered closed because of alleged discriminatory practices and other hidden barriers to trade. VIEs have become the sine qua non of a results-oriented trade policy that focuses on specific, concrete outcomes rather than on what proponents dismiss as free trade principles that rely on ineffective rules.

VIEs mandate that a country import a specific quantity of foreign goods in a specific industry, usually by setting a minimum import market share and often backed by the threat of tariff retaliation. As such, VIEs are the import counterpart to voluntary export restraints: while VERs set a quantitative ceiling on a country's exports of a given product to another country, VIEs set a quantitative floor on a country's imports of a given product from another country.[1]

---

1. VIEs entered the lexicon of trade policy after being first noted by Jagdish Bhagwati (1987), who coined the term to show their symmetry with VERs. Analysis of their implications was initiated in Bhagwati (1987, 1988, 1991) and has subsequently been extended, as discussed below.

1

Although VERs are generally considered harmful to the economic welfare of the importing country because they restrict trade, VIEs are more difficult to judge because their ostensible purpose is to expand trade in the face of alleged foreign trade barriers. As a result, VIEs have provoked sharp debate: either they are heralded as a positive, concrete step toward achieving a free trade outcome by gaining greater sales for U.S. exporters, or they are scorned as a step toward cartelized, managed trade and export protectionism through government-fixed market shares.

Primarily because of their apparent trade-expanding nature and the erroneous but widely held view that more trade is necessarily beneficial, VIEs have gained some legitimacy as a policy tool. According to government advisory groups on trade policy, some analysts at Washington think tanks, and even a few policy-oriented academics, VIEs have a rightful place in U.S. commercial diplomacy. But several VIE advocates also acknowledge the serious risks the policy may entail, in particular the danger that, by setting aside reserved market shares, VIEs will carve up foreign markets and further deteriorate the open multilateral trading system.

Despite these caveats, the Clinton administration has been attempting to use import targets as a key component of its trade strategy vis-à-vis Japan. In continuing negotiations with Japan arising from the July 1993 U.S.–Japan framework agreement, the administration has proposed using VIEs for the dual purposes of (1) reducing the bilateral trade imbalance by means of aggregate import expansion and (2) gaining greater market access by overcoming alleged informal barriers to trade in particular sectors.

This essay takes a critical look at VIEs as they have been commonly advanced by their proponents. Chapter 2 briefly reviews the context in which VIEs have appeared in the U.S. trade policy debate. Chapter 3 considers VIEs as means of expanding U.S. exports more broadly to reduce the bilateral trade deficit with Japan and the U.S. current account deficit. Chapter 4 addresses the more potent arguments that VIEs are necessary as aggregate and as sectoral measures to open up the Japanese market. Chapter 5 considers the U.S.-Japan experience with the VIE for semiconductors, an experience that suggests several lessons for those who desire a more general use of import targets. (An analytical appendix examines the question of how VIEs affect competition in the importing country's market.)

To anticipate the major conclusions, summarized in chapter 6, the monograph argues that VIEs are not an appropriate response to foreign trade practices that are allegedly unfair. When such practices can be identified, direct measures to remove or to mitigate them should be undertaken. When such practices cannot be identified, VIEs should also be avoided: because they are so arbitrary, they lack a plausible economic foundation and risk promoting, not competition, but the formation of cartels. VIEs are inherently discriminatory trade measures that take us away from the objective of an open multilateral world trading system. The slight probability that they might sometimes produce good results must be set against the far greater probability that they will bring harm, making their use an unwise policy option. VIEs are just another bad trade policy idea.

TWO

The Current Debate
over VIEs

In a curious reflection of the American character, the United States—despite its relative insulation from the world economy for many decades—has always been unusually disturbed by the specter of unfair foreign trade practices. This anxiety dates at least from the late nineteenth century and was enshrined in the reciprocity provisions of the McKinley Tariff of 1890. This act authorized the president to impose retaliatory duties against foreign countries that maintained unreasonable or discriminatory tariffs on U.S. products.

The U.S. agenda was not simply establishing fair trade; such provisions were also designed to gain preferential access for U.S. goods in Latin American markets.[1] Fair trade and reciprocity have long been a

1. As David Lake (1988, 101) points out, "The essential objective of these agreements was to gain an advantage in the Latin American markets at the expense of European producers." The general reciprocity provision in the McKinley Tariff reads much like section 301: "Whenever and so often as the President shall be satisfied that the government of any country producing and exporting sug-

theme of U.S. commercial policy; the United States has never been comfortable with free trade, especially on a unilateral basis. Since the Reciprocal Trade Agreements Act of 1934 and the early tariff-cutting negotiating rounds under the General Agreement on Tariffs and Trade (GATT), the United States has always insisted on the reciprocal reduction of trade barriers.

Section 301 Cases

Concern over reciprocity and market access abroad intensified in the 1980s, when the large U.S. merchandise trade deficit was matched by the realization that the country was no longer preeminent in many manufacturing sectors.[2] This generated intense political pressures to use the unfair trade (antidumping) laws or voluntary export restraints to alleviate the severe import competition that afflicted many industries. In 1981, for example, Japan was persuaded to

---

ars, molasses, coffee, tea, and hides, raw and uncured, or any of such articles, imposes duties or other exactions upon the agricultural or other products of the United States . . . he may deem to be reciprocally unequal and unreasonable, he shall have the power and it shall be his duty to suspend" the duty-free treatment of goods from "such designated country."

2. Jagdish Bhagwati and Douglas Irwin (1987) analyze the factors underlying the renewed emphasis on reciprocity in U.S. trade policy. Drawing a parallel with Britain at the end of the nineteenth century, they highlight the role of the diminished giant syndrome in the impassioned emphasis on reciprocity in trade that affected both countries as they faced the rise of new competitors in world trade.

adopt a VER on automobile exports to the United States, a trade restraint that dramatically increased the price of Japanese (and European) cars to U.S. consumers.[3]

The Reagan administration recognized that creating new barriers to imports was undesirable but was forced to accommodate many political pressures for import restrictions. In September 1985, however, the administration began a concerted effort to shift emphasis away from closing the U.S. market to imports toward measures that would open up foreign markets to U.S. exports. In undertaking the less objectionable task of reducing the foreign trade barriers that impeded U.S. exporters, what had been a rather obscure provision of U.S. trade law—section 301 of the Trade Act of 1974—rose to prominence.

Section 301 allows U.S. firms to petition the Office of the U.S. Trade Representative for remedial action against any "act, policy, or practice of a foreign country [that] is unreasonable or discriminatory and burdens or restricts United States commerce." If a

---

3. The VER proved a highly inefficient mechanism of transferring income from domestic consumers to domestic producers because consumer costs vastly exceeded domestic producer benefits. The main beneficiaries of higher automobile prices were the Japanese (and European) automakers who captured scarcity rents: Japanese automakers reaped more than $2 billion in 1982 alone, while their European counterparts also raised their prices, to capture $1.5 billion that year. It was also a highly inefficient and regressive jobs program: highly paid unionized workers were supported out of the pockets of workers elsewhere in the economy, at a cost per job "saved" of roughly $180,000 in 1982. These figures are taken from Elias Dinopoulos and Mordechai Kreinin (1988).

section 301 petition is accepted, the USTR undertakes negotiations with the foreign government to remove the "unreasonable or discriminatory" policy, with the threat of tariff retaliation hovering in the background should the negotiations fail.[4]

Early section 301 cases construed its scope as limited to attacking an official government policy or practice that was "unjustifiable," meaning any policy that is "inconsistent with or denies benefits of a trade agreement with the United States." The scope of the statute, however, was gradually expanded by amendments in 1979, 1984, and 1988 to encompass any other "unreasonable" act, policy, or practice that is "not necessarily in violation of or inconsistent with the international legal rights of the United States, [but] is otherwise deemed to be unfair and inequitable." Under the Omnibus Trade and Competitiveness Act of 1988, for example, the denial of "fair and equitable market opportunities, including the toleration by a foreign government of systematic anticompetitive activities by private firms or among private firms in the foreign country that have the effect of restricting, on a basis that is inconsistent with commercial considerations, access of United States goods to purchasing by such firms," is an actionable section 301 offense. Also included are the inability to set up a business enterprise and the persistent denial of worker rights in a given country.

VIEs are closely related to the export-oriented section 301. Section 301 cases often result in real market openings, in the sense that government trade barriers are removed and an outcome closer to free

---

4. See Jagdish Bhagwati and Hugh T. Patrick (1990) for a detailed discussion of section 301.

trade is obtained. As a result of a section 301 case in 1988, for example, Japan agreed to replace its import quotas on oranges and orange juice with a lower, nondiscriminatory tariff. J. Michael Finger and K. C. Fung (1994) determined that thirty-eight of fifty-one total liberalizations obtained under section 301 through 1992 were officially nondiscriminatory.

In other cases, the unilateral nature of the section 301 process—the United States extracts nonreciprocal concessions from other countries—opens the door to demands for preferential market access by U.S. exporters. When the U.S. government welcomes such demands as acceptable remedies to a particular case and when a foreign government acquiesces to such pressure, VIEs—government-fixed market shares allocated to particular countries or companies—are one possible outcome. In the second section 301 case ever filed, for example, a complaint from the United Egg Producers and American Farm Bureau about a Canadian quota on the import of U.S. eggs was resolved simply by doubling the quota for U.S. produce without changing the total import quota. In such cases, section 301 may detract from the objective of an open world trading system based on nondiscrimination and brings about, not free trade, but trade diversion.

Early VIEs

Indeed, the first and most important VIE came as a direct outgrowth of a section 301 case. In 1985, the Semiconductor Industry Association filed a section 301 complaint against Japan for supporting informal barriers to the importation of foreign semiconductor devices. While no formal government policies were ever identified, the SIA maintained that the U.S. market share in Japan (at roughly 10 percent) was implausibly low compared with the U.S. market share in third markets. The SIA further argued that the market structure in Japan and the buying preferences of Japanese firms, both resulting from government policy, hindered the sales efforts of foreign producers. The association called for an "affirmative action" scheme from the U.S. government to help it penetrate the Japanese market in the face of hidden, invisible trade barriers. As a result, in a 1986 agreement the United States forced the Japanese government to help ensure that foreign suppliers would obtain 20 percent of Japan's semiconductor market within five years. This controversial market share target was laid out in a secret side-letter, which read:

> The Government of Japan recognizes the U.S. semiconductor industry's expectation that semiconductor sales in Japan of foreign capital-affiliated companies will grow to at least slightly above 20 percent of the Japanese market in five years. The Government of Japan considers that this can be realized and welcomes its realization. The attainment of such an expectation depends on competitive factors, the sales efforts of the foreign capital-affiliated companies, the purchasing efforts of the semiconductor users in Japan and the efforts of both Governments.[5]

In 1991, a new U.S.-Japan semiconductor trade agreement (United States 1991, 3) was reached; it

---

5. See Douglas A. Irwin (1994) for the full text of the side-letter and for a detailed discussion of the semiconductor agreement.

explicitly recognized the market share target and extended the deadline for reaching 20 percent by one year:

> The Government of Japan recognizes that the U.S. semiconductor industry expects that the foreign market share will grow to more than 20 percent of the Japanese market by the end of 1992 and considers that this can be realized. The Government of Japan welcomes the realization of this expectation. The two governments agree that the above statements constitute neither a guarantee, a ceiling, nor a floor on the foreign market share.

Although foreign semiconductor producers achieved a 20.2 percent share of the Japanese market in the fourth quarter of 1992, the market share target has been a source of continual friction between the United States and Japan. The foreign share fell to nearly 18 percent in the first three quarters of 1993— at which point U.S. Trade Representative Mickey Kantor called for "emergency consultations"— although that share jumped back over 20 percent in the fourth quarter of 1993.

A second operative VIE between the United States and Japan concerns automobile parts and resulted, not from a section 301 case, but from presidential action over Japan's perceived closeness to outside parts suppliers. During President Bush's visit to Japan in January 1992, the United States and Japan agreed to a Global Partnership Plan of Actions. Part of this package was the pledge by Japanese automobile manufacturers to purchase a specific amount of U.S.-made auto parts. The text of this pledge (United States 1991, sec. 12, pt. 2, p. 1)—which, unlike the semiconductor agreement, was not officially sanctioned by the Japanese government—read:

(a) Automobile parts procurement by US manufacturing facilities of Japanese affiliates from US suppliers is expected to more than double from about 7 billion dollars in FY 1990 to about 15 billion dollars (in real terms) in FY 1994.

(b) Seen in terms of percentage of local procurement in the total purchase of parts, the percentage is expected to increase from about 50% in FY 1990 to about 70% in FY 1994. By contrast, the percentage of imports from Japan is expected to decrease from about 50% to about 30%.

(c) In making these procurements, special consideration will be given to the US parts industry, which is currently under a difficult situation.

Clinton's VIE Goals

The semiconductor and auto parts VIEs are the only two formal VIEs recognized by the United States, and they are unique in their special circumstances. The Clinton administration, however, is attempting to broaden the reach of VIEs to other sectors and thus to institutionalize the use of quantitative indicators or market share targets as part of U.S. trade policy toward Japan. Spurred by the apparent success of the market share provisions of the semiconductor agreement, the Clinton administration has embraced it as a model of a "results-oriented" trade agreement, that is, one that focuses on specific outcomes in which there is "measurable success" on the basis of explicit targets and quantitative indicators.

11

This new emphasis on explicitly mandated results has arisen from the perception that previous market-opening initiatives with Japan have failed because the standard process- or rules-based approach is too easily undermined or subverted by Japanese countermeasures. The Clinton administration's stated approach envisions VIEs for the twin purposes of (1) reducing the Japanese current account surplus (and thereby the long-standing U.S. bilateral trade deficit with Japan) and (2) improving market access and combating opaque methods of protection in specific sectors. On the trade deficit, as reported in the April 28, 1993, *International Trade Reporter,* Secretary of Commerce Ronald Brown has stated that "the only logical way . . . to address that problem [the trade imbalance] is to have some measurable results, to have some targets. . . . When there have been no targets, when we have not had a results-oriented approach, no progress has been made." On market access, according to the December 6, 1993, *Washington Post,* U.S. Trade Representative Kantor has argued that "if you don't get real numbers in an agreement, you'll effectively have nothing."

Since taking office, the Clinton administration has sought to establish specific import targets with Japan but has encountered strong resistance from the Japanese government. In July 1993, the United States and Japan established a Framework for a New Economic Partnership as a guide for new negotiations over structural and sectoral issues. The structural negotiations aim "to achieve over the medium term a highly significant decrease in [Japan's] current account surplus and at promoting a significant increase in global imports of goods and services, including the United States." The sectoral negotiations seek "substantially to increase access and sales of competitive foreign goods and services through market-opening" measures in Japan. These negotiations are designed to have agreements in place within a year's time (summer 1994) and to use "objective criteria, either qualitative or quantitative" to evaluate progress in meeting the agreement. According to President Clinton's interpretation, reported in the July 14, 1993, *International Trade Reporter,* the two countries "have agreed what the outcome of the negotiations needs to be: tangible, measurable progress."

In the framework negotiations, the Clinton administration had strongly pushed for quantitative benchmarks such as VIEs to ensure compliance and to realize market access and has even threatened to impose and to monitor specific, quantitative benchmarks unilaterally. The United States demanded early agreements on the use of quantitative market indicators in four sectors: (1) auto parts and automobiles, (2) medical equipment, (3) telecommunications equipment, and (4) insurance. Table 2–1 indicates the U.S. negotiating position in these areas. Japan has refused to adopt quantitative benchmarks and insisted that such standards would constitute guaranteed market shares in violation of free trade principles. The Japanese government fears accountability for (and perhaps even retaliation over) the failure to meet import targets because of factors beyond its control. Japan does not wish to commit to a 30 percent annual increase in foreign telecommunications equipment sales, for example, when its economy remains mired in recession. The two countries failed to conclude any early agreements. The stark failure of the February 1994 meeting between President Clinton and Prime Minister Morihiro Hosokawa drama-

TABLE 2–1: U.S. Demands in Framework Talks with Japan

Area	Goal	Measures to Reach Goal
Auto parts and autos	20% annual increase, for four years, in auto parts sales to Japanese car makers in United States and Japan	1. Increase domestic content of Japanese cars made in North America to more than 75%. 2. Steadily increase numbers of Japanese car dealers selling foreign cars. 3. Ease car registration and inspection requirements.
Medical equipment	25% annual sales increase, for four years, to Japanese government	1. Early information about hospital purchasing plans. 2. Judge bids by "overall greatest value," not lowest price. 3. Track contracts awarded to foreigners.
Telecommunications equipment	30% annual sales increase, for four years, to Nippon Telegraph & Telephone and to Japanese government	1. Reform NTT purchase practices. 2. Earlier notice of bids. 3. Track contracts awarded to foreigners.
Insurance	General expansion of foreign sales, so Japan moves in line with other industrialized countries	1. Eliminate rules requiring companies to consult with competitors before introducing new products. 2. Measure how fast applications are approved. 3. Track approval rate for foreign applications.

Source: *Wall Street Journal*, February 14, 1994, p. A8.

tized the gulf that divides the two countries over VIEs and trade policy.

The administration's support for VIE-type policies has not been shared by many economists, who generally remain skeptical of or opposed to the government's setting quantities of traded goods. In this sense, VIEs have frequently been likened to VERs. Both VERs and VIEs are political responses to reducing bilateral trade frictions in particular sectors. VERs are a common response to the "problem" of "too many" exports of a particular product coming from a particular country; VIEs threaten to become a common response to the "problem" of "too few" imports of a particular product by a particular country. From the perspective of the country requesting trade relief, VIEs and VERs are merely two sides of the same coin: VERs fix the quantities of foreign exports, and VIEs fix the quantities of foreign imports to politically appropriate levels. Both VERs and VIEs are voluntarily adopted by a country only because it is threatened by more unpleasant actions imposed by the afflicted country if no measures are taken.[6]

Although VERs and VIEs are both quantitative

---

6. If Japan did not "voluntarily" agree to limit its automobile exports in 1981, for example, the United States would have imposed much more stringent restrictions on its exports, such as harsh tariffs, quotas, or domestic content requirements. With VIEs, if some "voluntary" measure to increase imports of semiconductors were not undertaken, Japan would have faced tariff retaliation or harsh antidumping duties against its exports to the United States. VIEs are less voluntary than VERs, however, because export restraints generate quota rents for domestic exporters, whereas import expansions diminish the market shares of domestic firms.

trade measures, VIE advocates argue that their underlying purpose is quite different: by limiting imports, VERs restrict trade and move away from free trade; by expanding exports, VIEs enlarge trade and supposedly move toward free trade in the face of some alleged foreign trade barrier. As Laura D'Andrea Tyson (1990, 180) has written, "Although it is hard to defend voluntary export restraints from an economic perspective, the economic case against the voluntary import expansion restraints is weaker and less well documented."

This uncertainty about the economic effects of VIEs is strikingly apparent in the most prominent VIE, the import market share targets in the U.S.-Japan semiconductor agreements. Analyzing the economic effects of the semiconductor VIEs is much like analyzing the effects of affirmative action in a case where discrimination has not been proved. The semiconductor industry never established that import barriers in Japan were really present. If there were no barriers, then the VIE was "export protectionism" for the United States: enforcement depended entirely on the Ministry of International Trade and Industry's forcing Japanese semiconductor purchasers to accommodate the market share target and to switch their purchases to foreign producers. If hidden trade barriers artificially reduced U.S. sales in Japan, a VIE might conceivably achieve conditions that might have existed under free trade.

Can the VIE provision in the semiconductor agreement be therefore viewed as a success? We postpone until chapter 5 further consideration of this VIE, but, in one sense, it is not surprising that the agreement "worked": stipulated targets can always, with appropriate enforcement actions, be satisfied. In another sense, it is indeed surprising that it worked: with no clearly identified obstruction to imports, enforcement depended on credible threats by MITI to change the purchasing practices of private Japanese firms. The welfare implications are somewhat ambiguous: U.S. producers are better off, Japanese producers worse off, and Japanese consumers may or may not be better off, depending on the efficiency of existing contracting relationships and the quality and price of U.S. semiconductors.

While the administration is clearly sympathetic to VIEs and may even be willing to pursue them without Japan's acquiescence, the precise form and method of implementing additional VIEs remain to be seen. But are there sound reasons for the United States to be pressing Japan to adopt VIEs in the first place? For this and related questions to be assessed, existing proposals and rationales for VIEs need to be canvassed to understand the circumstances under which VIEs have been advocated and the goals that they seek to achieve.

THREE

A Remedy for Trade Imbalances

The state of the U.S. merchandise trade balance—or, more broadly, the current account balance, which includes both merchandise trade and services and investment income—has been a concern to U.S. policy makers for more than a decade. In particular, the persistent U.S. trade deficit with Japan has been a source of bilateral tension since the 1970s. Officials of the Clinton administration maintain that Japan's trade surplus is a drag on the world economy, if not evidence that Japan's market is closed. Because the United States has aimed to reduce the deficit as much through actions by Japan as through its own, import targets are now relied on to achieve a desired current account and trade balance position.

The Clinton administration's objective in the framework negotiations has been to set targets capping Japan's current account surplus. The administration's main objective has been to persuade Japan to adopt a more "stimulative" fiscal policy stance in part through greater government purchases of foreign goods. Administration officials and others have stated that trade policies, such as aggregate import expansions, also contribute to reducing Japan's current account surplus. Henry Kissinger and Cyrus Vance (1988, 913–14) argued several years ago that the "American-Japanese dialogue must not be confined to mutual harassment and recrimination on an industry-by-industry basis," and, instead, both countries should "seek to establish overall [trade-related] goals and work toward them." Specifically, the United States should define a tolerable trade balance, and, "within that balance, Japan would have the choice of either reducing its exports or increasing its imports, thus removing the need for sector-by-sector industrial negotiations."

Once the underlying source of the U.S. current account deficit (and Japan's surplus) is understood, however, trade policy measures such as broad import targets can be seen as unconstructive. The effectiveness of such broad import targets depends entirely on whether they change the underlying determinants of the current account balance, namely, domestic savings and investment. And in using trade policy to affect these factors, policy objectives and policy instruments are grossly mismatched.

Domestic Finances

During the 1980s, when the United States experienced large current account deficits, economists repeatedly stressed that current account deficits are a macroeconomic phenomenon that reflect an imbalance between domestic savings and domestic investment. In countries such as the United States in recent

19

years, where domestic investment has exceeded domestic savings, this investment can be financed only
by borrowing from abroad. This source is recorded
in the balance of payments as a capital account surplus and means simply that the United States is a net
borrower from other countries: more U.S. assets are
sold to foreigners than foreign assets are purchased
by U.S. residents. Since the balance of payments must
always balance—the current account (trade in goods
and services) and the capital account (trade in assets)
must equal zero, by accounting definition—the capital
account surplus is just the mirror image of a current
account deficit.

Japan is the flip side of the U.S. case. At world
interest rates, the pool of Japanese savings exceeds
domestic investment and has been invested abroad;
this situation implies that Japan's capital account
deficit must be matched by a current account surplus.
Consider the dramatic shift in Japan's current account position from a $10.8 billion *deficit* in 1980 to a
$20.8 billion *surplus* in 1983 (and one that grew to
peak at $87.0 billion in 1987). This shift did not
reflect a rapid closing of Japan's market to imports or
an increase in "unfair" trade practices but simply
reflected the liberalization of Japan's capital account
transactions. Before 1980, most developed countries
(including Japan) restricted the international mobility
of short-term capital as a legacy of the Bretton Woods
system of fixed exchange rates. With the December
1980 enactment of the Foreign Exchange and Foreign
Trade Control Law, all outward movement of capital
from Japan was freed. This permitted Japanese savings to leave the country in search of higher returns
in world financial markets. The massive amounts of
Japanese foreign investment implied large capital ac-

count deficits (and conversely current account surpluses) for Japan through the 1980s.[1]

Kissinger and Vance and many others wrongly attribute the source of Japan's bilateral trade surplus with the United States to "the current superior productivity and long-range planning of Japanese industry." The U.S. bilateral trade deficit indicates that Japan is a net lender to the United States: the high savings rate in Japan generates funds that are transferred partly to the United States in capital account transactions that require offsetting movements to the current account. While the precise mechanisms by which the current and capital accounts move in tandem are complex—and depend on such factors as exchange rates, relative goods prices, expected asset prices, and income changes across countries—the key point is that trade policy cannot change the external imbalance unless it also alters the underlying savings and investment choices of households, firms, and the government in an economy.[2]

Domestic Solutions

Thus, trade policy per se does not directly affect the state of the balance of payments: countries do not

1. See chapter 11 of Takatoshi Ito (1992) for a discussion of Japan's external balances in the 1980s.

2. Attributing trade deficits to exchange rates correctly identifies one mechanism by which such imbalances can arise. Proposals to establish exchange rate targets (as in C. Fred Bergsten and Marcus Noland [1993]), however, seemingly forget that floating exchange rates are not direct policy instruments but an endogenously determined relative price that cannot be affected without underlying changes in monetary and fiscal policies. These underlying

run trade surpluses as a result of their "unfair" trade practices, and trade deficits do not reflect greater "openness" to others. Trade policy is an ineffectual way of achieving a particular current account position because it does not directly affect the fundamental macroeconomic determinants of the current account. As such, VIEs are clearly a misguided policy instrument with which to effect such an adjustment of external balances.

This simple lesson—at a time when the U.S. current account deficit is much smaller as a percentage of the gross domestic product than it had been in the mid-1980s—now appears to be lost once again as the U.S. deficit begins to creep upward. If reduction in the current account deficit is accepted as an objective of U.S. economic policy, it directly points the way toward efforts that either promote domestic savings or, more directly, reduce dissaving on the part of the federal government by reducing its fiscal deficit.[3] The U.S. fiscal deficit is a substantial component of the gap between domestic savings and domestic investment, and its reduction can contribute to reduction in the current account deficit. As the federal government's fiscal deficit shrank from 4.7 percent to 2.4 percent of GDP between 1986 and 1989 (from roughly $200 billion to $124 billion in nominal terms), for example, the deficit on trade in goods and

---

macroeconomic policy changes are almost never explicitly discussed in such exchange rate proposals.

3. Despite the lip service paid to the first measure, it implies a reduction in consumption out of each dollar of income, something political leaders are understandably reluctant to stress or promote.

services also fell from 3.1 percent to 1.6 percent of GDP.[4]

Unlike congressmen such as Richard Gephardt, who routinely advocates VIEs ostensibly to reduce Japan's current account surplus, the Clinton administration is more focused on getting Japan to pursue a "stimulative" fiscal policy to reduce its surplus. Such an act would affect the macroeconomic determinants of the external accounts, but the objective of reducing Japan's surplus is questionable. The current environment is a particularly poor one in which to force Japan to reduce its external surplus. Japan is the only major industrial country with a substantial current account surplus; its reduction would deprive the rest of the world of its lending, would tend to raise world interest rates, would diminish investment projects at the margin, and would thereby harm the medium-term prospects for economic growth in North America and Europe. Rather than placing the burden of external adjustment on Japan and attacking Japanese thrift and fiscal prudence in the hopes of inducing the Japanese to act on our behalf, the United States should reduce its fiscal deficit for its own benefit. To ask Japan to run budget deficits similar to our own to soak up its vast domestic savings is tantamount to exporting U.S. fiscal profligacy.

Indeed, nothing is inherently bad about running either a bilateral trade or a current account deficit (although these may reflect other policies that might require changes). This is implicitly recognized in policy discussions of the U.S. trade deficit, which fail to identify the adverse consequences of that deficit except the vague notion that unsustainable deficits

---

4. Calculated from data in United States 1994, apps.

threaten the underlying stability of the world economy's financial system. To the extent that the U.S. trade deficit with Japan is considered unsatisfactory because it serves as a lightning rod for protectionist pressures, the appropriate policy is, once again, underlying changes in U.S. fiscal policy that will reduce the current account deficit and will keep domestic interest rates low.

Yet even if the United States were to achieve a current account balance, the bilateral trade imbalance with Japan would likely persist, partly because of the particular financing needs of Japan's trade structure; Japan's imports of raw material and fuel from Southeast Asia and the Middle East must be paid for by trade surpluses with other industrial countries. Balanced trade between the United States and Japan could be achieved overnight if all capital flows between them—all borrowing and lending activity and trade in financial assets—were immediately prohibited. But mutually advantageous trade does not depend on bilateral trade balancing, and this draconian step would shut down the multilateral settlement of bilateral trade balances and would be disastrous for the world economy.

Fortunately, there is broad agreement in the current debate, even among many proponents of VIEs, that alleged informal Japanese trade barriers do not inhibit a U.S. current account adjustment and that aggregate import expansion policies are an inappropriate policy for reducing the trade and current account deficits. Most of the current debate concerns VIEs as aggregate or sectoral measures to open up Japan's market, where the problem of Japanese trade barriers is somewhat better defined and import targets can be more clearly justified.

FOUR

Opening "Closed Markets" in Japan

While trade policies are an ill-conceived means to redress external imbalances, such policies in the United States and Japan do affect the composition of bilateral trade and, hence, domestic resource allocation and, ultimately, the economic welfare of both countries. Given the widespread perception that government restrictions and private exclusionary practices exist as formidable import barriers in Japan, it is much less surprising that VIEs have gathered more support as broadly or narrowly defined import targets to open up the Japanese market more effectively.

Broad or Sectoral Targets?

One proposal for broadly based import targets comes from Rudiger Dornbusch, who is skeptical about whether sectoral negotiations can achieve real progress in opening Japan. He (1990, 120) flatly states that the Japanese economy "remains basically closed in manufactures trade and, of course, in agriculture" and therefore that the United States should aim to increase market access broadly in Japan. Dornbusch (124) advocates that

> a target should be set for growth rates of Japanese imports of U.S. manufactures. Monitored on three-year moving averages, Japanese manufactures imports from the United States should grow at an average (inflation-adjusted) rate of 15 percent a year during the next decade. . . . An automatic and effective sanction mechanism should be put in place to ensure a timely response and a complete Japanese understanding that adjustment is required.

These sanctions should consist of "across-the-board surcharges on Japanese imports, triggered automatically and proportionate to the shortfall of Japanese import growth."

This proposal is an extreme instance in which process does not matter at all, and results are the ultimate end, although the mechanism by which this is achieved is left unstated and therefore deemed irrelevant. Dornbusch remains unperturbed that Japan might simply divert trade from other countries toward the United States; in that case, "one would hope that Europe would make the same demand" for a share of Japan's trade. (Other countries with no bargaining power would presumably be left on their own to negotiate over the remaining scraps of the market, an issue to which we return.)

In contrast to aggregate import expansions, sectoral VIEs have received support from several quarters in the United States. The Advisory Committee on Trade Policy and Negotiations (ACTPN), a group led by prominent business leaders, issued a report to the USTR in January 1993 calling for "temporary quantitative indicators" to counteract "invisible barriers" to imports in Japan. These indicators would "simulate what both sides expect would happen in a particular sector if Japanese businesses and consumers made purchase decisions on the sole basis of commercial considerations—price, quality, and delivery." The report states that the benchmark indicator would be removed once imports hit the proper level but that "failure to achieve the indicator within a pre-agreed time frame would call for internal review in the United States and/or bilateral discussions to determine what additional measures are necessary to achieve the result, possibly leading to retaliation."

The Council on Competitiveness, another business-dominated group, has similarly endorsed a new trade policy stance against Japan, one that emphasizes specific outcomes. The council (1993, 19) maintains that although rules-oriented trade agreements "are always more desirable," "results-oriented agreements that entail concrete market access commitments, such as foreign market share targets, are sometimes necessary" and "would appear to have greatest relevance for Japan." In studying the semiconductor trade agreement with Japan, the council (55) concludes that "a results-oriented trade policy, including market access goals, can sometimes provide a useful tool for measuring and leveraging fair market access when process-oriented approaches are not successful."

Support for sectoral VIEs has also come from outside the business community. Before joining the Clinton administration, Laura D'Andrea Tyson argued that there is a legitimate role for managed trade arrangements such as VIEs in high-technology sectors. Claiming that there is an absence of internationally agreed upon rules governing trade in high-technology sectors and extensive intervention in these sectors by other industrialized countries, she argues (1990, 151) that "an outcome approach may be essential if barriers to critical foreign markets are causing serious harm to domestic producers in important high-technology industries." Indeed, she (1990, 181) argues that

> if the target applies to a country and an industry in which there is ample evidence of market closure—as is surely true for Japan in the semiconductor industry—and if the target applies broadly to imports from all foreign suppliers or the most important foreign suppliers rather than imports from a specified supplier—as is true in the semiconductor agreement—then the import expansion restraints may enhance competition rather than cartelize world markets.

Because of the singular economic importance of high-technology industries, VIEs "cannot be discounted as a reasonable policy response. . . . If the objective of policy is to increase market access abroad, voluntary import expansion restraints may be a useful tool."[1]

Criticisms of Japan

While generally quite skeptical of VIEs, C. Fred Bergsten and Marcus Noland (1993, 196) propose that "VIEs do appear to be suited to a particular kind of problem that the United States sometimes faces in its

---

1. See also Tyson (1992, 264ff).

dealings with Japan." They advance two cases in which VIEs are defensible. First,

> foreign providers of industrial intermediates or capital goods wanting to sell into the Japanese market. . . . sometimes find that their entry is blocked by the contracting relationships of the vertical *keiretsu* system. . . . these long-standing relationships were developed in the context of what was essentially a closed system. Once these firms become major players in the international economic system, there is a clear political (and arguably an economic) rationale for developing a broader, more inclusive, *international* web of relationships. . . . It may act as a prod to internationalize the *keiretsu.*

Second, echoing Tyson,

> there may be cases, such as semiconductors and supercomputers, where the issues are such that internationally agreed-upon rules of competition are unlikely to be formulated in the politically relevant time frame. . . . In these cases, VIEs may make some sense as a mechanism to force the adaptation of a system that was developed in the closed, policy-distorted environment of Japan in the 1950s and 1960s. A VIE could then be considered as a *temporary* compensatory policy to move the Japanese system closer to a free trade equilibrium.

Mandated market openings by means of import market share targets are the "avenue by which this inherently discriminatory structure in Japan is made compatible with an open international trade system" but should be considered "only in the case of industrial intermediates."[2]

The argument that Japan's trade barriers require a special U.S. response in the form of sectoral VIEs is predicated on two claims: (1) Japan is an unusually closed market with pervasive informal trade barriers and exclusionary practices that distort the composition of its foreign trade and (2) the traditional "process-" or "rules-oriented" approach of insisting on equal access fails in effectively opening up the market. From these premises, VIE proponents reach the conclusion that trade policies requiring specific, quantitative outcomes are necessary to overcome or to compensate for hidden barriers and can even erode them by introducing new competition in the Japanese market. Yet the first premise is grossly exaggerated, and the second is altogether inaccurate.

Japan's transparent barriers to trade, such as tariffs and quotas, are generally insubstantial except for agricultural goods. While these formal barriers for the latter are still a source of dispute—for example, Japanese restrictions on the importation of rice—the more intractable and elusive "informal" bar-

---

2. Bergsten (1993) later distinguished VIEs as good managed trade from VERs as bad managed trade; he endorsed the semiconductor trade agreement as a "proper use of managed trade to promote exports." "VIEs may be necessary in markets that deny access to foreigners through a web of opaque exclusionary practices that cannot be addressed by the usual tools of trade policy," he concluded, because previous policies have left a "profound legacy of market closure." But see the reply by Bhagwati (August 24), the response of Bergsten (October 15), and the additional rejoinder by Gary Saxonhouse (October 22), all in letters to the editor of the *Financial Times*.

TABLE 4–1
SHARE OF MERCHANDISE TRADE IN GROSS DOMESTIC PRODUCT, 1992
(percent)

United States	8.2
Japan	7.8
European Community	8.6

NOTE: Merchandise trade figures are average of exports and imports divided by GDP. European Community figures exclude intra-EC trade.
SOURCE: Organization for Economic Cooperation and Development, *Monthly Statistics of Foreign Trade,* January 1994.

riers—either hidden or discriminatory government practices and private business behavior—are more frequently cited as hindering the penetration of foreign manufactured goods. Because evidence on these factors is necessarily sketchy or anecdotal, the importance of these informal barriers cannot be readily assessed.

It is often argued that Japan's imports are too low compared with other industrialized countries and that this constitutes indirect evidence of the distortionary impact of hidden, informal barriers to Japan's trade. Table 4–1 indicates that the average share of trade in Japan's GDP is not substantially different from that share in the United States and the European Community. Because of its current account surplus, Japan's share of imports in its GDP is lower than in the United States and the European Community. But because Japan's trade ratio is similar to these countries on average, simple ratio comparisons fail to

31

TABLE 4–2

COMPOSITION OF INTERNATIONAL TRADE BY
COMMODITY, 1992
(percent)

Commodity	United States		Japan		Germany	
	Ex-ports	Im-ports	Ex-ports	Im-ports	Ex-ports	Im-ports
Food	9	8	2	16	5	10
Raw materials	9	11	0	34	3	11
Manufactures	81	82	98	50	92	79

SOURCE: See table 4–1.

provide convincing economic evidence of market closure.

The composition of Japan's trade by commodity, in contrast, is quite different from that of the United States and European Community (table 4–2). Japan's underlying economic attributes, primarily its scarcity of arable land and natural resources, ensure that a large proportion of imports will be food, fuel, and raw materials. By necessity, therefore, Japan is a processing economy: Japan must export manufactured goods to pay for the imports of food and energy. Japan's great success over the past century has been to encourage the accumulation of physical and human capital and to adopt modern technology such that its exports have shifted from unskilled labor-intensive goods to more advanced products. But no compelling evidence exists that the volume or composition of Japan's external trade is significantly different from what should be expected of any country given Japan's natural and accumulated resource endowments, distance from trading partners, and average degree of protection.[3]

This renders blanket statements like U.S. Trade Representative Kantor's—"Japan's markets are closed by any measure you may choose"—completely absurd.[4] A tendency for Japan's distinctiveness and closeness to be exaggerated, however, does not mean that import barriers do not exist.[5] These barriers are of legitimate concern to U.S. trade policy makers. The real question is whether process- or rules-oriented U.S. trade policies are effective in reducing those barriers. Proponents of VIEs argue that because the major impediment to sales in Japan is "structural," negotiations that fail to deal with the different structure of Japan will not yield "results."

Past Exercises in Trade Liberalization

Past trade liberalization exercises under the auspices of the GATT, in fact, succeeded in bringing about

---

3. As C. Fred Bergsten and William R. Cline (1987, 92) point out, "Japan shows no special aberration of low imports that might be attributable to high but intangible protection, after taking account of country size, natural resource endowments, and transportation costs. And although the share of manufactures in Japan's total imports is low, there are sound reasons of comparative advantage to expect this pattern." See also the discussion and critique of various econometric studies of Japan's trade pattern in Gary Saxonhouse (1993).

4. Quoted in the *Financial Times*, February 11, 1994, p. 15.

5. Barriers do indeed exist, but there is no persuasive evidence that they distort Japan's trade to a substantially

"results" in increasing Japan's imports: J. Michael Finger (1976) presents evidence that Japanese imports responded to the Kennedy Round tariff reductions in the same way as other developed countries' imports. The existing orientation of U.S. trade policy with Japan, including bilateral sectoral negotiations without import targets, has also worked to bring about "results." A recent study by Peter L. Gold and Dick K. Nanto (1991) finds that U.S. exports to Japan of products discussed in bilateral negotiations (section 301, market-oriented sector-specific talks and the like) grew substantially faster than total exports to Japan. The negotiations over liberalizing Japanese policy in particular sectors apparently added about $5 billion to exports above and beyond the average rate of increase of U.S. exports to Japan. Gold and Nanto conclude (1991, 6) that "the trade data do not appear to support the so-called revisionist critics who claim that normal trade concessions by Japan do not lead to increases in U.S. exports."

Such market openings have produced much greater export sales than commonly anticipated at the time—precisely because the negotiations focused on specific, identifiable trade barriers that lent themselves to policy changes by the Japanese government. As C. Fred Bergsten and Marcus Noland (1993, 195 n. 12) point out, had the United States settled for a market share target in many of these cases—such as cigarettes, beef, and citrus—not only would it have failed to address the underlying trade barrier, but the target would have drastically understated the actual demand for U.S. goods under true liberalization: "In

---

greater degree than such barriers in other industrialized countries so as to treat Japan as a gross outlier.

hindsight, it is very difficult to believe that trade officials could have obtained negotiated [that is, managed trade] solutions in any of these cases that would have been nearly as advantageous to U.S. interests as the market solution obtained through genuine liberalization."

Therefore, the two premises behind the advocacy of VIEs—the unusually closed Japanese market and the failure of trade liberalization to yield results in Japan—are unsubstantiated. Yet perceptions remain that the traditional approach of U.S. trade policy toward Japan has proved ineffectual because in certain contentious sectors, negotiations have been persistently difficult.[6] In these sectors, VIE proponents claim that pervasive, informal trade barriers defy traditional negotiated settlements about rules and therefore require VIEs. Much has been claimed about these hidden trade barriers, but a specific description is needed to assess their validity and to prescribe appropriate treatments.

Trade Barriers in Japan

What, specifically, are these much discussed but rarely identified barriers? Bergsten and Noland (1993, 72) enumerate them:

> The methods of import control include discriminatory networks of affiliated firms *(keiretsu);* administrative guidance on the part of government officials to intimidate importers; misuse of customs procedures

---

6. The equally protracted negotiations over setting additional import targets clearly indicate that VIEs are not a quick fix.

and product standards, testing, and certification requirements to discourage imports; incomplete enforcement of patent and trademark rights; government procurement procedures that advantage domestic suppliers; and restrictions on the distribution channels for imported products, to name a few.[7]

While the authors do not advocate VIEs except in the case of the *keiretsu,* the specificity of this list is useful in thinking about the calls from business groups and others for explicit import targets. With the exception of the *keiretsu,* what is readily apparent from scanning this list of "methods of import control" is that they are not hidden at all. With the exception of the *keiretsu,* each of these methods involves explicit and identifiable governmental policy, obstructions created by Japanese government bureaucrats to protect special interest groups. Consider briefly the problem of each of these "methods of import control" and the appropriate remedy, saving the *keiretsu* issue for last.

The first is administrative guidance and intimidation. The anecdotal nature of evidence about this factor complicates assessment of how much significance should be attributed to it. Administrative guidance, however, has grown increasingly ineffective and unimportant in the postwar period, as the instruments of government control, such as foreign exchange allocation or export licenses, have disappeared from the economic landscape. While such guidance and intimidation are clearly objectionable—

---

7. This list is similar to that in USTR 1993 and in United States 1994, 218.

and by their nature can probably never be proved—a sense of proportion should be maintained: an equal number of anecdotal horror stories can be told about the discretionary application of U.S. antidumping law and the harassment of foreign exporters by the Department of Commerce. Whatever the case, if bureaucratic power is sufficient to support intimidation against importers, it seems odd to ask these same bureaucrats to negotiate a VIE that (1) they appear to have no interest in doing and (2) would only strengthen their power over resource allocation in the industry. The long-run national interest of the United States is better served by reducing, rather than strengthening, the power of the bureaucrats in MITI and the Ministry of Finance.[8]

Bergsten and Noland next identify "misuse of customs procedures and product standards" as a barrier against imports. Several well-known tales of abuses have received much attention, partly because of the sometimes ridiculous Japanese explanations for them, such as the unsuitability of American aluminum baseball bats, the inappropriateness of Western skis for Japanese snow, harmful and unsafe apples from the state of Washington (the recent alar controversy notwithstanding), and other well-publicized examples. Once again, it is difficult to assess the importance of these examples, but there is certainly no reason to ignore them. These problems do not call out for a market-fixing VIE to tame the offending Japanese bureaucrats but are best handled through impartial procedures at the GATT for settling disputes and through improved GATT disciplines on

8. See the *Economist*'s leader, "Mismanaged Trade," January 22, 1994.

customs procedures and valuation practices. The recent apples case illustrates that agreements on better procedures for preimportation inspection requirements can also yield a satisfactory outcome. Thus, no compelling reason demands an import market share target rather than a direct removal of the objectionable government policy.

Enforcement of patents and trademarks is a problem not just in Japan but in many other countries. The GATT has dealt with this situation through negotiations on trade-related intellectual property (TRIP) and is clearly the proper avenue for pursuing this goal. VIEs are surely an inappropriate way to deal with international differences over patent rights and, at any rate, would not solve the underlying problem.

Discriminatory government procurement practices, particularly in telecommunications equipment and construction services, have been a continual source of bilateral friction.[9] Discriminatory government practices are clearly not unique to Japan and are frequently the subject of international trade con-

---

9. Since the 1970s, for example, the United States has objected to the discriminatory purchase of telecommunications equipment by the then government-owned Nippon Telegraph & Telephone Corp. (NTT) and signed a bilateral agreement under which Japan agreed that NTT must solicit competitive bids. A sense of proportion is needed in telecommunications equipment procurement. Just over a decade ago in the United States, AT&T (a regulated but private firm) was vertically integrated and purchased all its telecommunications equipment from its subsidiary, Western Electric, thereby discriminating against and excluding from the market not only all foreign telecommunications producers but all domestic producers as well.

flict, as the recent exchange of retaliatory tariffs between the United States and the European Community illustrates.[10] The assumption, in this case as in others, that small foreign market shares in Japan are sufficient evidence of closed markets is weak. When USTR negotiators complained that Japan's government purchased only 1.6 percent of its telecommunications equipment from foreign firms, the Japanese negotiators responded that the comparable figure for the United States is only 0.3 percent (Reid 1993).

Government procurement policies in the United States, Japan, and the European Community should be put on the negotiating table. GATT's government procurement code should be strengthened. VIEs would not only hinder the process of finding a uniform set of international rules on government procurement but would not liberalize the market in a desirable way.

The above policies in Japan and elsewhere are either explicit trade barriers or discriminatory government policies that are legitimately the subject of international negotiations. In all cases, these policies

---

10. In early 1993, the United States imposed $19 million in retaliatory sanctions against the European Community for a directive that allowed EC utilities to reject comparable bids (3 percent price margin) from non-EC tenders (those with less than 50 percent EC content) and allowed them to reject bids from non-European suppliers. The EC counterretaliated against $15 million of U.S. equipment, pointing out the many Buy American provisions in the United States that give domestic firms a 25–100 percent preferential price margin against foreign rivals and laws mandating that 20 percent of all federal contracts go to small- and medium-sized domestic firms. *International Trade Reporter,* February 24, 1993.

should be subject to discussion in a multilateral forum such as the GATT or in bilateral or sectoral negotiations if appropriate. VIEs are clearly an inferior, second-best outcome: they do not fundamentally resolve the underlying problem of bureaucratic obstacles for U.S. exporters to Japan.

The *Keiretsu*

Finally, we come to the most contentious "invisible" trade barrier, the *keiretsu*. The *keiretsu* as a trade issue is on a different plane from the others because it raises the question, not of government barriers to trade, but whether the organization of private firms in one country can be considered an anticompetitive trade practice by another country. Indeed, the *keiretsu*—as the strictly private practices of Japanese firms or particular forms of business organization—must be distinguished from specific, identifiable government policies that discriminate against foreign goods. Complaints about the *keiretsu* focus on practices that the government does not directly control. Therefore, the international obligation of the government in administering or affecting a change in these practices to suit another government is not clear.

Although any definition is necessarily subject to qualification, the term *keiretsu* loosely describes a host of interfirm relationships and affiliations of varying degrees of formality in Japan. These ties are often categorized into several groupings. Horizontal *keiretsu* are composed of numerous firms operating in different markets tied together by cross-firm equity holdings and associated with a large commercial bank

40

that serves as their main source of capital.[11] Vertical *keiretsu* describe similarly close stock-holding relationships between firms at various stages of production or the long-term subcontracting arrangement of a firm with its suppliers of intermediate goods. Distributional *keiretsu* refer to manufacturers that organize and control the wholesale and retail distribution channels of their products.

The vertical *keiretsu* have stimulated the most suspicion and debate in terms of trade policy. They are frequently believed to constitute a discriminatory, exclusionary, and preferential purchasing arrangement that artificially blocks the participation of outside firms. Therefore, according to VIE proponents, import targets are equivalent to an affirmation action policy that will force the *keiretsu* to source outside the Japanese market.

The ACTPN report, for example, stresses that "more progress needs to be made, particularly in . . . dealing with private anti-competitive practices (e.g., exclusionary buying preferences within the *keiretsu*) which are restricting market access for imported products," and concludes that "affirmative inclusion of foreign suppliers is the best way to reverse the trade restrictive impact associated with these practices." Bergsten and Noland (1993, 196–97) similarly believe that VIEs "should only be considered in the case of industrial intermediates" when foreign firms "find that their entry is blocked by the contracting

---

11. The United States is fairly unique in not permitting financial institutions to hold equity in other corporations. Despite this freedom in many other countries such as Germany, Japan is singled out by U.S. trade policy makers for not having such regulations.

relationships of the vertical *keiretsu* system." Bergsten and Noland state that "it makes no sense to propose [VIEs] for consumer products or final goods of any sort."

These rather calm statements conceal the tremendous heat that the *keiretsu* have generated.[12] Yet on a conceptual level, the current obsession with the vertical *keiretsu* is simply bizarre. There is nothing illegitimate, illegal, or unfair about the Japanese system of vertical supply relationships, which are simply a particular form of private business organization. Firms can organize their chain of production in one of three ways: spot market or arm's-length transactions with various suppliers, long-term contracting relationships with subcontractors, or full vertical integration, whereby inputs are produced within the confines of the firm. The vertical *keiretsu* is simply an affiliation or long-term contract between a firm and its input suppliers, and thus is an intermediate stage of business organization between spot market relationships and vertical integration. In this sense, the *keiretsu* are inherently "discriminatory" and "exclusionary" because, as Paul Sheard (1992, 35) notes, "this sense of 'exclusionary' is almost the definition of a long-term contract." Such contracts or vertical ties, at least for the duration of the contract or links, obviously "exclude" outsiders—outside domestic and foreign firms alike. If a *keiretsu* firm were entirely

---

12. Chalmers Johnson (1990, 17) insists that the *keiretsu* are nothing but "the rigging of a market system in order to cause it to achieve political goals." Robert Lawrence (1991) argues that Japan "under-imports" in *keiretsu* sectors, although the comments by Gary Saxonhouse at the end of that paper are instructive.

vertically integrated, then the market would be completely "closed"—indeed, would not exist—because intermediate goods would be sourced entirely within the firm.

There exists a well-defined economic efficiency rationale for the vertical *keiretsu* behavior.[13] This intermediate degree of integration gives a firm the advantage of close, long-term cooperative ties with its suppliers, not the fixed, permanent ties that might reduce the competition that forces responsiveness among suppliers. Since the 1970s, management gurus in the United States have touted the *keiretsu* organization as worthy of emulation. As an alternative to the perceived rigidity of vertical integration and loose informality of the spot market, the *keiretsu*, with its intense competition among subcontractors and related flexible just-in-time inventory system, have been viewed as a source of Japan's economic success. To label the *keiretsu*, as Bergsten and Noland do, as a "method of import control" is thoroughly misleading;

---

13. Sheard (1992, 38–39) describes this rationale: "By facilitating the making of credible commitments that curb opportunistic behavior, long-term contracts can provide incentives for transacting parties to make valuable specific investments. Many long-term transactional relationships in Japan can be viewed in this light: workers making firm-specific investments in human capital in the context of lifetime employment guarantees; suppliers making specific investments in physical or organizational capital in order to supply customer-specific inputs to purchasers; main banks expending resources to accumulate customer-specific information and information-processing capacity. Commitment is the essential ingredient in long-term contracting. . . . commitment and exclusion are two sides of the same coin in this context."

it smacks of a deliberate, government-created or -sanctioned means of reducing import penetration rather than one particular form of business organization.

But do the *keiretsu* facilitate, or are they manifestations of, anticompetitive (monopolistic or predatory) behavior by Japanese firms? The problem, Sheard notes (1992, 21), is that the "mechanisms by which *keiretsu* are supposed to reduce competition or impede entry are not spelled out. Being specific about this is important because it allows their plausibility in terms of economic logic to be checked." After an exhaustive examination of the issue, Sheard concludes (1992, 3, 23) that "popular discussion associating *keiretsu* with anticompetitive behavior lacks a solid foundation in economic analysis," in part because "as long as the final goods market is competitive forms of vertical relations can have no anticompetitive implications." Any firm that deliberately discriminates against more competitive outside suppliers suffers a cost disadvantage that harms its competitive position against other rivals. To incur this cost willingly, a firm must find some offsetting cost advantage to this form of organization. But Japanese final-goods producers hardly appear saddled with inefficient suppliers and therefore act at a disadvantage with respect to their foreign competitors.

Empirical evidence in David E. Weinstein and Yishay Yafeh (1993) also indicates that the *keiretsu* are not anticompetitive cartels but are so highly competitive that the *keiretsu,* and even other firms in the sectors with a *keiretsu* presence, are associated with low price-cost margins. Small markups are hard to reconcile with the usual results of cartel-like behavior, and the low import share in *keiretsu* sectors is more likely a consequence of intense domestic competition rather than of exclusionary practices.[14]

The problem with treating corporate organization and behavior as an artificial trade barrier is not just that it (in Sheard's words) "blurs the analytical distinction between different sources of closeness and is a source of considerable confusion in the debate." It is by no means clear that these private practices are inefficient and discriminatory and therefore deserve a negative connotation. No compelling, underlying efficiency rationale for attacking the *keiretsu* has been established. This is perhaps why Bergsten and Noland argue that there is a clear "political" rationale for expanding the web of international relationships in Japan, rather than elaborating on any potential economic benefits of breaking up the *keiretsu*. Without such rationale, VIEs aimed at the vertical *keiretsu*—as in the case of semiconductors, which is discussed shortly—will force involuntary contracting in Japan: purchasers will be directed to abandon preferred sources of supply for another, a task that can be accomplished only under the watchful eye of MITI.

Forgotten in much debate about the *keiretsu* is the greater tendency to vertical integration in U.S. firms than among comparable Japanese firms. Figure 4-1 illustrates that, for a wide variety of manufacturing industries, Japanese firms rely on subcontracting to a greater extent than their American counterparts. In the automobile industry, it is frequently noted that Japanese firms typically outsource or subcontract

---

14. The low price-cost margins reflect not higher costs because of *keiretsu* preferences but lower prices because of the interests of main banks in promoting the sales growth of the firm.

FIGURE 4–1

COMPARISON OF SUBCONTRACTING IN SELECTED INDUSTRIES,
JAPAN AND THE UNITED STATES, 1977

(percent)

(a) Industries with High Dependency on Subcontracting

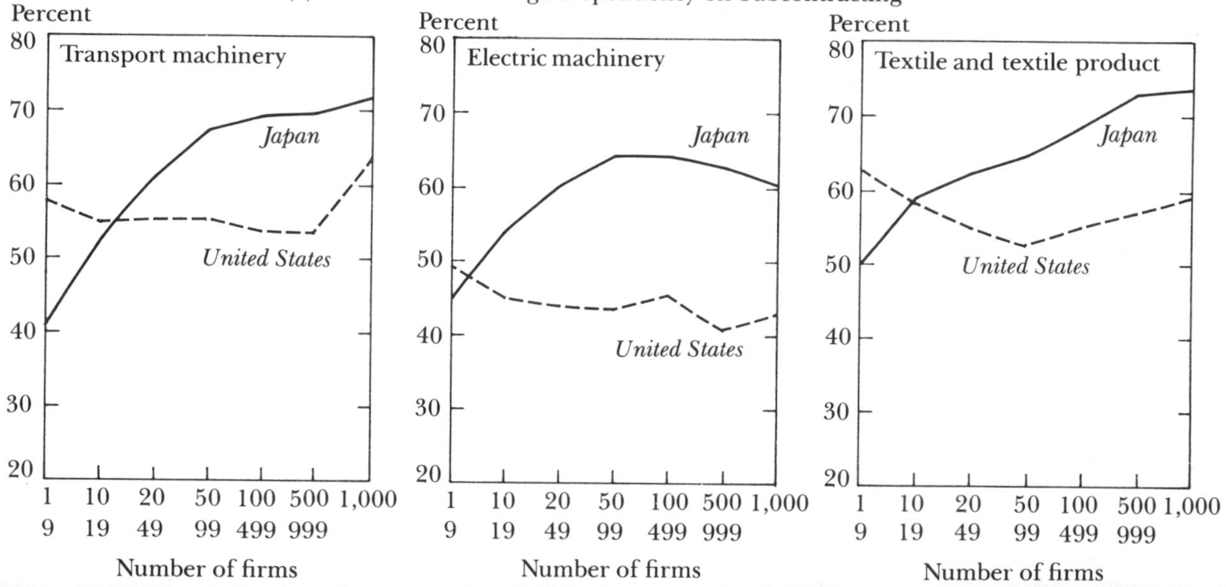

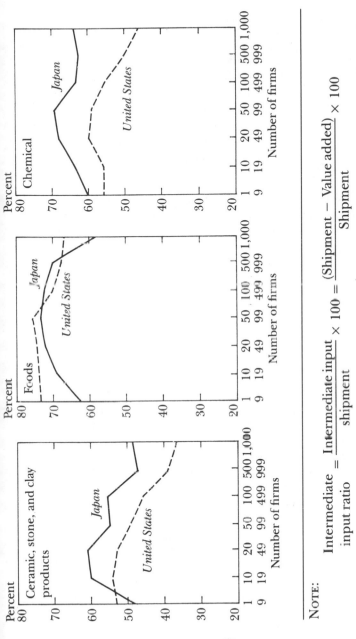

NOTE:

$$\text{Intermediate input ratio} = \frac{\text{Intermediate input}}{\text{shipment}} \times 100 = \frac{(\text{Shipment} - \text{Value added})}{\text{Shipment}} \times 100$$

SOURCES: For Japan, Ministry of International Trade and Industry, *Kogyo Tokeihyo* (Census of Manufactures) (1977). For the United States, *Census of Manufactures* (1977).

SOURCE: Yaginuma (1993), p. 14.

about 75 percent of production costs, whereas U.S. firms subcontract about 50 percent. In this case, there is a greater degree of "exclusion" of possible suppliers by General Motors than by Toyota.[15] From this perspective, Gary Saxonhouse (1993, 38) aptly raises the question: "Is it really interesting for the United States and Japanese trade negotiators to be arguing about practices that could be resolved legally with simply more vertical integration in Japan? Why is formal vertical integration in the United States better or fairer than informal integration in Japan?"

One industry in which more formal vertical integration is greater in Japan than in the United States is semiconductors. A plausible efficiency rationale exists for integration in certain segments of this industry because of the learning-by-doing, dynamic-scale economies that arise in semiconductor production. U.S. merchant firms (that is, nonintegrated firms that sell semiconductors on the open market) have complained bitterly about the vertical ties among Japanese semiconductor firms and computer and consumer electronics firms. But imagine the reaction in the United States if Japanese producers complained to MITI and the Commerce Department about their inability to sell to one of the world's largest consumers of memory chips—IBM—because of that firm's exclu-

---

15. A curious feature of the complaint that U.S. automobile parts producers do not have access to the Japanese market (despite the greater degree of subcontracting there) is that major U.S. auto producers have large equity stakes in major Japanese firms: in late 1991, for instance, GM owned nearly 40 percent of Isuzu, Ford held more than 20 percent of Mazda, and Chrysler held 10 percent of Mitsubishi.

sionary, discriminatory, and preferential practices in producing its own chips internally rather than relying on subcontractors.

This analogy suggests that the activities of foreign private firms should not be subject to trade negotiations until the ramifications and implications of such negotiations for the organization of domestic firms in the United States are understood as well. If there is evidence that Japanese firms are engaged in anticompetitive practices, the appropriate remedy should be more vigorous competition policy and antitrust enforcement rather than managed trade. The problem is that international codes on restrictive business practices are weak. The United States killed the International Trade Organization, predecessor of the GATT, because its regulations in this area were thought to impinge too much on basic domestic antitrust issues such as resale price maintenance, vertical restraints, and the like. There is little consensus on such issues today in the United States. The United States can reopen international discussion on harmonizing domestic competition policies but should be prepared to accept reciprocity: the United States might be required to change its antitrust policies on vertical integration or financial policies on equity holding by banks.

There are legitimate and justifiable instances in which the United States can and should complain about access to the Japanese market. These cases should be subject to adjudication by GATT panels, bilateral negotiation, and possibly even section 301 actions.[16] Employing VIEs, however, is tantamount to

---

16. One needs to distinguish between section 301 actions to enforce treaty-sanctioned trading rights and those to secure new, unreciprocated concessions. The latter aim

giving up, forgetting about the objective of genuine trade liberalization, and simply settling for a share of the market.

In fact, the mere presence of a VIE suggests that the "liberalization" may not be genuine because the U.S. negotiators could not pinpoint a policy or practice that could be meaningfully described as a government trade barrier. This was the case with the most prominent VIE—semiconductors, a classic instance in which the U.S. industry and government failed to identify any Japanese policy that blocked imports. The problems that the United States and Japan have encountered with this agreement indicate the problems that afflict VIEs more generally.

---

is problematic; see the discussion in Bhagwati and Patrick (1990).

FIVE

Lessons from the U.S.-Japan Semiconductor VIE

Before 1975, imports of semiconductors into Japan were restricted by formal quotas and prior approval requirements; foreign investment was so strictly regulated as to be essentially forbidden. These restrictions were liberalized in 1975; afterward, few formal governmental trade barriers remained in place. Indeed, Japan's tariffs on semiconductors were eliminated in concert with the United States in 1985. Despite these reforms, the U.S. share of the Japanese semiconductor market scarcely budged. The Semiconductor Industry Association charged that the market opening was a sham and claimed that informal nontariff barriers continued in Japan after 1975. According to the SIA, MITI undertook active countermeasures to undermine the liberalization and thereby prevented foreign semiconductor producers from making inroads into the Japanese market.

In 1985, the SIA filed a section 301 petition with the USTR, complaining about their lack of market access in Japan. The group could not identify explicit government trade barriers but maintained that "structural barriers" in Japan's market were an impediment to foreign entry. The SIA contended that the Japanese government condoned anticompetitive practices, such as reciprocal trading or tie-in relationships among firms, promoted "Buy Japan" attitudes, and used administrative guidance to thwart the 1975 liberalization.

Because the alleged import barriers were "hidden," the SIA could provide only circumstantial evidence that such barriers even existed. The industry group frequently pointed to the market shares held by U.S. producers in various other regions. In 1984, for example, U.S. semiconductor producers accounted for 83 percent of sales in the U.S. market, 55 percent in the European market, 47 percent in the other (primarily Asian) markets, but only 11 percent in the Japanese market. By the SIA's (1985, 2) interpretation, "these trade [market share] figures, coupled with Japan's protectionist heritage in microelectronics, strongly suggest that market barriers still exist in Japan." As a result, they requested an "affirmative action" plan enforced by the Japanese government to increase its market share in Japan.

A major shortcoming of the SIA's petition was that, unlike Motorola's early cellular phone difficulties in facing a government monopoly (Nippon Telegraph & Telephone Corp.), no specific government restraint was ever identified: there was no smoking gun. Beyond vague claims about the policies and attitudes of the Japanese government and firms, essentially the SIA resorted to identifying the structure of the Japanese market as a barrier to trade. The structure of the Japanese semiconductor market was indeed different from that in the United States: as Japan's output of consumer electronics (such as color televisions, videocassette recorders, laptop computers, and the like) exploded in the late 1970s and 1980s, major producers of such goods found it advantageous to produce semiconductors themselves rather than to purchase them on the open market. U.S. semiconductor firms had difficulty selling to Japanese firms using semiconductors partly for the same reason that they had difficulty selling to IBM; like IBM, Japanese producers opted for vertical integration, to produce semiconductors in house or from affiliated subcontractors based on long-term contracts, rather than to acquire them in arm's-length transactions.[1]

Furthermore, the SIA figures on country shares in regional markets could not prove the existence of import barriers. In fact, an alternative explanation for those shares was consistent with no Japanese "unfair" trade practices: U.S. producers dominated the U.S. market, Japanese producers dominated the Japanese market, and U.S. producers essentially split European and Asian markets with other producers, holding a slightly higher share in Europe because of long-standing direct investments in Europe behind a tariff barrier that kept out Japanese imports. The Japanese share in the United States—which at this time was similar to the U.S. share in Japan—may have

---

1. The difficulties of U.S. producers in Japan may also have been due to a quality gap. A well-publicized Hewlett-Packard study in the early 1980s indicated that the failure rate of U.S.-made semiconductors was six times higher than that of Japanese-made semiconductors.

been restricted by a discriminatory U.S. semiconductor distribution network.[2]

Since no obvious import barriers were ever identified, and the actual market shares provided inconclusive evidence of barriers at best, any foreign market share target in Japan was destined to be arbitrary. In this particular case, the market share target resulted from a downward political adjustment to the finding of a study commissioned by the SIA—hardly an independent source of information—purporting that the U.S. industry would capture 30–40 percent of the Japanese market under free competition. A nominally secret side-letter to the 1986 U.S.-Japan semiconductor trade agreement specified that the Japanese government "recognized the U.S. semiconductor industry's expectation" that the share of "foreign capital affiliated firms" would reach 20 percent in Japan within five years. This market share target applies primarily to U.S. firms and not necessarily to exports of U.S. production: exports to Japan from NEC and Fujitsu production in the United States are excluded from the target, while Texas Instruments production and sales in Japan are included in the target.

Under the 1986 semiconductor agreement, the Japanese government was ultimately responsible for ensuring that the market share target of 20 percent

---

2. In the early 1980s, there was an "unspoken ban on Japanese franchises" among U.S. distributors because, on marketing Japanese chips, U.S. firms would cancel all contracts with that distributor. The distributors had the "dictum that large houses will not take on the Japanese so long as they are supported by domestic suppliers" (Bambrick 1985).

for foreign producers was met. The enforcement of the agreement posed a serious challenge to MITI: without a formal governmental policy that impeded imports, such as procurement policy or standards setting, the Japanese government had no direct policy instrument—and thus no immediate leverage—to ensure the satisfaction of the VIE target and hence adherence to the agreement. MITI had to use moral suasion and administrative guidance with the implicit (or perhaps even explicit) threat of penalties or official disfavor to diminish the resistance of domestic semiconductor purchasers to foreign products. While several large Japanese firms using semiconductors already purchased about 20 percent of their semiconductors from U.S. vendors at the time of the 1986 agreement, numerous smaller purchasers were well below this target.[3] In seeking to prevent these firms from free riding on the purchases of the large companies, MITI conducted extensive surveys of the purchasing plans of all semiconductor users to monitor and to evaluate progress toward the 20 percent target. MITI was enforcing an affirmative action policy against the resistance of the private sector. This created so much tension between the industry and the government that MITI officials later swore never to adopt such explicit market share targets again.[4]

The U.S. retaliation against Japan in early 1987

---

3. MITI complained to the United States that, while it had some influence over the larger firms, its leverage over the smaller firms was much weaker.

4. Newspaper reports in 1987 suggested that reluctant Japanese firms would buy foreign semiconductors to satisfy MITI and then dispose of the unwanted goods by dumping them in Tokyo Bay.

for noncompliance with the agreement strengthened MITI's ability to pressure recalcitrant firms into adhering to the market share target. In the end, the foreign market share in Japan finally reached 20.2 percent in the fourth quarter of 1992, the deadline specified in the 1991 renegotiated agreement. In 1993, however, the share fell to nearly 18 percent before rebounding above 20 percent in the last quarter. The fluctuation in the market share has been a source of ongoing tension between the two governments.

According to the SIA, the 1986 accord had its biggest impact in promoting greater cooperation between its members and the members of the Electronic Industries Association of Japan. The proliferation of joint research, production, and sales ventures between U.S. and Japanese firms bears witness to the extensive forms of cooperative cross-firm ties that have arisen since 1986. Greater opportunities for U.S. producers have been established in Japan, particularly in obtaining design-in contracts, and the agreement possibly served to induce a more focused sales effort by U.S. companies in Japan. But cooperative cross-firm ties and Japanese accommodation of U.S. sales also create the opportunities for tacit collusion, and the effect of these cooperative alliances on competition in the semiconductor industry is extremely hard to establish.

The semiconductor agreement worked in the sense that a stipulated import target can be met by appropriate actions by the Japanese government. This was accomplished, however, by expanding the scope of government influence in the Japanese semiconductor industry. In signing the 1986 agreement, the Japanese government believed that it had merely "recognize[d]" and "welcome[d]" the realization of "the U.S. semiconductor industry's expectation" that foreign sales would grow to 20 percent of Japan's market. When, six months after the agreement was signed, the United States announced its tariff retaliation for noncompliance, the Japanese government came to the unwelcome realization that the U.S. government held it strictly responsible for satisfying movement toward that particular market share. This accounts for Japan's current reluctance to putting any numerical benchmarks or market share figures—let alone explicit targets—on paper. From Japan's perspective, welcoming the realization of an expectation implies strict responsibility for ensuring the realization of that expectation, even when "the two governments agree that the above statements constitute neither a guarantee, a ceiling, nor a floor on the foreign market share," as the 1991 accord states.

Several lessons emerge from the experience with the U.S.-Japan VIE in semiconductors that will affect the possible implementation of VIEs in other sectors.

VIEs Are Arbitrary

The semiconductor VIE suggests that import targets are inherently arbitrary on several dimensions. If explicit government restrictions are not apparent, one can never be sure whether hidden or informal barriers do, in fact, exist. To deduce the presence of import barriers based on comparative market share analyses alone is an approach fraught with interpretive difficulties. Was the low U.S. semiconductor market share in Japan in the early 1980s due to unfair government trade practices and an exclusionary market structure or simply to a different structure of

57

semiconductor demand in Japan (from the consumer electronics industry, which the United States largely lacked) and the significantly higher failure rate of U.S. chips? Is the low U.S. share of Japan's automobile market due to hidden trade barriers or to the failure of the U.S. industry (until recently) to produce quality automobiles under 2,000 cubic centimeters (80 percent of Japan's market) with right-side steering?

Low import market shares alone cannot be accepted as prima facie evidence of discriminatory practices. As journalist Michael Prowse recently put it, in "A Prussian in the White House" (in the *Financial Times,* February 21, 1994), "Suppose France analysed US wine consumption and found an unfair bias in favour of inferior Californian brands. Would Mr Clinton be happy if President Mitterrand unilaterally set a numerical target for increased US imports of French Burgundy?"

This brings out a fundamental conceptual weakness of VIEs: because of the enormous difficulties in assessing what accounts for low import shares, there is no reliable economic basis for determining the foreign market share without the alleged discriminatory practices. No satisfactory methodology can calculate the target market shares, and the choice of the market share target is therefore inherently arbitrary and devoid of any serious economic foundation. In guessing what the foreign market share "should be," U.S. trade negotiators inevitably rely on information provided by interested parties. In reality, they do not bother to undertake any independent evaluation.

Advocates of VIEs propose market share targets as "temporary" indicators, yet the choice of the VIE's time frame is arbitrary. No one familiar with the trade policy experience of the postwar period is sanguine that VIEs will not be perpetuated. The SIA (1990, 33) once argued that "after a 20 percent level had been achieved, [the] foreign share would float to an appropriate level based on competitive merit and without further government targets. . . . [the target was] a threshold from which market forces would then take over and operate." Yet when the foreign share of Japan's semiconductor market reached 20 percent at the end of 1992, the industry association urged that the import target be maintained, if not increased. Certainly, the lessons of trade policy for other industries—textiles and apparel, sugar, and others come to mind—suggest that, once established, government support tends to become institutionalized and perpetuated.

The mere stating of a number—a target, even if backed by nothing—creates an "entitlement" environment for VIE-favored foreign firms in which any shortfall is a ground for complaint. There is intense focus every quarter that the foreign share of Japan's semiconductor market is calculated: any increase is hailed by Japan as progress; any lapse is noted with concern by the SIA and the USTR. The 1991 semiconductor agreement states, "The two governments agree that the above statements [about the foreign market share] constitute neither a guarantee, a ceiling, nor a floor on the foreign market share." Yet the SIA and USTR act as though it is a guaranteed floor and issue ominous press releases or demand consultations after any fall in the foreign market share. After a recent complaint from the United States, one MITI official was quoted as saying in the *Wall Street Journal,* December 8, 1993, "The more the U.S. side overemphasizes this decline in the market share, the more we are convinced that we will never again negotiate a semiconductor-type arrangement."

The particular commodities that come under the scope of a VIE are arbitrary. Industries such as semiconductors, telecommunications equipment, and computers encompass a wide variety of differentiated goods. The broader the industrial aggregate chosen for an import target, the more arbitrary the VIE becomes in its inclusion of different types of goods. U.S. producers are not necessarily competitive in all product segments of these industries, and not all of those segments in which U.S. producers are competitive may be appropriate to the needs of the foreign market. Over the arbitrary timetable, the competitive position of U.S. firms could shift or the requirements of the Japanese market may change, regardless of informal import barriers.

All these arbitrary elements to VIEs are not without economic significance or consequence. The arbitrary nature of VIEs means not simply that the setting of such import targets lacks any economic basis; it also raises important issues for their enforcement. To be credible, the VIE must be backed by the implicit or explicit threat of retaliation against Japan for noncompliance. As Bergsten and Noland (1993, 195) point out, "The VIE puts the exporting country in the position of making a decision whether to retaliate on the basis of factors outside either government's control, such as changes in the composition of demand or technological developments (as in the case of the STA [Semiconductor Trade Arrangement]) or exchange rate changes." This is clearly undesirable and adds to the inherent uncertainty surrounding the import target: is failure to satisfy the import target evidence of Japanese recalcitrance or was the target set at the wrong level for the wrong commodity or has the composition of demand in the foreign market simply changed in the intervening period?

The government setting of market shares, simply put, is a bad basis for administering U.S. trade policy.

VIEs Diminish Competition

In contrast to other government trade interventions such as VERs, VIEs are frequently defended as measures that would expand trade, increase competition, and promote a free trade outcome. Tyson (1990, 181) suggests that "the import expansion restraint may enhance competition rather than cartelize world markets" and (1992, 265) may "destabilize the institutional and informal arrangements that impede foreign access." Bergsten and Noland (1993, 196) view VIEs as a "*temporary* compensatory policy to move the Japanese system closer to a free trade equilibrium." Indeed, a critical issue in the debate over VIEs is whether setting import market share targets when hidden trade barriers are alleged will increase competition and move firms toward a free trade outcome or will reduce competition and foster collusion.

Experience with the U.S.-Japan semiconductor agreement indicates that, if no explicit government barriers have been identified, enforcement of the VIE target is unlikely to enhance competition.[5] The agreement has clearly altered the nature of competi-

---

5. The antidumping provisions of the U.S.-Japan agreement clearly reduced competition in the semiconductor market. These provisions acted in effect as a VER and facilitated collusion among Japanese exporters. See the discussion in Tyson (1992) and Kenneth Flamm (1993).

tion in the semiconductor industry as indicated by the proliferation of joint ventures between U.S. and Japanese firms since 1986. Some industry analysts suspect that the manifold joint ventures have diminished the high degree of rivalry between U.S. and Japanese firms and the competitive vigor of Japanese firms. Officials at USTR have noted, for example, that the complaints of U.S. semiconductor producers about their Japanese rivals diminished with the announcement of each joint venture.

Proponents of VIEs suggest that import targets increase competition because foreign firms must compete for the new shares. But do firms really compete for new market shares? If a certain percentage of the Japanese market is set aside for foreign firms, if Japanese producers are restricted in their home sales (as opposed to VERs, which restrict their foreign sales), does this enhance competition? Certainly, if foreign producers are imperfectly competitive, these firms may recognize their bargaining power vis-à-vis their Japanese customers and not really compete but negotiate for additional market shares.

In forcing Japanese firms to accommodate the sales of U.S. firms, VIEs present the additional danger of being captured by the initial beneficiaries of affirmative action in Japan. These firms have a vested interest in securing their own profits by declaring the VIE a success and discouraging other foreign firms from entering the market. In this case, VIEs do not increase competition but merely create rents for the first few foreign firms that are beneficiaries of the affirmative action.

Fears of such co-optation were raised in the context of the U.S.-Japan semiconductor accord shortly after the announcement that foreign producers had achieved over 20 percent of Japan's semiconductor market in the final quarter of 1992. A Texas Instruments spokesman stated that the industry would "be happier with less government involvement" in overseeing market access since they had now become "part of the Japanese *keiretsu*" (Hamilton and Davis 1993). Texas Instruments was one of the few firms with long-standing direct investments in Japan and therefore had advantages over other U.S. rivals in selling to Japan. Although the SIA quickly disavowed any lapse in the 20 percent market share target, questions were raised about whether Texas Instruments and perhaps other firms were seeking to preserve their position in the Japanese market against new competition.

More generally, even if additional firms are represented in the market as a result of a VIE, their mere presence does not necessarily increase competition. As Avinash Dixit (1990, 188–89) has pointed out,

> There is no general, simple connection between numbers [of firms] and competition in industrial organization. In this context, if A and B agree to have fixed shares of each other's market, that is not competition. For competition, A needs to fear that if he raises his price, B will win over some of A's customers. The share agreement precludes this possibility. . . . management [of trade] does imply cartelization.

An analytical appendix to this monograph indicates why there is a foundation for Dixit's concern. This appendix considers the simplest possible model of imperfect competition to highlight the strategic reactions of a Japanese and a foreign firm to the market share target. This analysis shows that, in the presence of an invisible foreign trade barrier, even if an import target is set to match the market shares under free trade, the VIE fails to increase competition and to replicate free trade. Instead, the VIE proves to be a facilitating practice that fosters collusion, just like VERs. The act of the Japanese government forcing the Japanese firm to reduce its domestic sales and to share the market with its foreign rival gives rise to a more coordinated, and therefore a more collusive, interplay between the two firms. In the end, competition is not enhanced; only profits are shared.

The analysis also raises important political economy issues; namely, even if the Japanese government has the ability to remove the invisible impediment to U.S. entry, the Japanese firm may lobby instead for a collusion-facilitating VIE rather than for free trade.[6] In fact, both firms would prefer a VIE to free trade because collusion allows them to maximize joint profits. Under some circumstances, the credible announcement of such market share agreements might be able to alter competition in a market in a way that fosters collusion. And even if such share agreements are temporary, they risk persistently altering the degree of market competition by fostering the formation of collusive mechanisms.

In cases where no specific government impediments to trade have been identified for reform, VIEs

---

6. The Japanese firm does not want the VIE in the first place. Because the VIE is clearly involuntary (unlike all VERs), VIE enforcement becomes a key issue. But forced to choose between free trade and a VIE, the firm prefers the latter.

are likely to become managed trade in the worst sense. They will inherently require substantial government intervention to become effective because the government of the importing country has no direct policy instrument with which to effect the desired change.[7] With unidentified hidden barriers, a VIE's effectiveness necessarily depends on explicit and continual administrative or enforcement actions by the government. If the U.S. products are not truly competitive on some dimension, this practice merely compounds enforcement difficulties. Further, imports must be rationed and allocated among domestic consumers to satisfy the market share target. Where a specific governmental policy is at issue, by contrast, negotiations can aim to remove the policy that blocks imports and the market adjusts automatically with competition and without any further government action.

VIEs Are Discriminatory

VIEs need not be formally discriminatory. The market access provision of the semiconductor agreement was officially nondiscriminatory since it referred to "foreign capital-affiliated" semiconductor firms, not simply to U.S. firms. Indeed, in 1988, the European Community lost a GATT panel decision challenging

---

7. This feature of VIE-enforcement illustrates an oddity of U.S. trade policy: the United States never seems concerned about the mechanism by which "voluntary" bilateral agreements are carried out and acts as if the foreign government can solve the problem by fiat. The United States never explicitly states how it expects a foreign government to realize its obligation, and enforcement is always simply left to the foreign government.

the agreement as a violation of the most-favored-nation clause. The GATT ruled that the provision did not necessarily entail discrimination against non-U.S. suppliers.

Yet concerns about whether the market share target applies in a nondiscriminatory fashion to all foreign producers or just to U.S. producers as a preferential market opening will be a part of any managed trade arrangement such as VIEs. In the auto parts agreement arising from President Bush's trip to Japan in 1992, explicit reference is made just to "U.S. suppliers," as noted. Despite formal assurances to the contrary, there is ample reason to believe that VIEs will continue explicit discrimination in favor of the United States. The 1993 framework agreement between the United States and Japan states that "Benefits under this Framework will be on a Most Favored Nation basis." But in negotiating a new automobile and auto parts VIE, the Clinton administration has proposed "specific expectations" for greater Japanese imports, not of any and all foreign automobiles, but specifically those produced by American-owned companies (not even Japanese or European transplant production in the United States) (see Pollack 1993).

As Jagdish Bhagwati (1991) has pointed out, even if preferences for U.S. firms are not explicit, the Japanese government and Japanese firms will interpret the VIE as encouraging imports principally from the United States. Faced with an involuntary import expansion, Japan would feel pressure to appease the complainant and to divert trade toward the United States. Japan recognizes that the pressure to import more arises almost exclusively from the United States. Unlike the removal of a formal barrier to trade, the market share target will remain underfilled unless the Japanese government pressures Japanese firms to increase their foreign purchases in a way that reduces tensions with the United States.

Even if Japan were able to administer the VIE in a nondiscriminatory way, other countries would interpret the VIE as a preference to U.S. firms. Despite the GATT panel ruling that the 1986 semiconductor agreement did not discriminate against European firms, the European Community has pressed for its own market share targets in Japan. The European Electronic Components Manufacturers Association noted that Europe's estimated world semiconductor market share outside Europe and Japan is roughly 5 percent, while its share in Japan is less than 1 percent. In the summer of 1992, after the renegotiation of the U.S.-Japan semiconductor agreement in 1991 had explicitly put the market share target in the text of the agreement, European producers—believing that they had been cut out of trade missions sponsored by the Electronic Industry Association of Japan and the SIA—demanded their own market share target of 5 percent in Japan (Lineback 1992).

VIEs are therefore bilateral trade policies with multilateral repercussions. The setting of import targets by two countries—even if, in principle, on a most-favored-nation basis—is perceived by those excluded as fixing market shares to the detriment of others. In this way, bilateral trade restrictions tend to spread; just as a single VER can lead to export restraints with several countries, a single VIE can lead to import targets with several countries. In both cases, quantitative trade restrictions or expansions tend to carve up world markets by political fiat and pressure. With

VIEs, smaller and weaker countries with less political and economic influence are left behind to fight over the remaining scraps of the market. This situation not only pits one rival against another in seeking target shares of another's market, it further retreats from the reciprocal process of reducing trade barriers under multilateral rules and therefore threatens the GATT system.

From its perspective, the United States is not always interested in providing the international public good of increased market access in Japan. It is interested in satisfying domestic interest groups and, to use a phrase from the semiconductor case, "making the cash registers ring" for U.S.-owned firms. Any unilateral U.S. action against unfair foreign trade practices will be subject to political pressures for preferential or discriminatory access for U.S. producers. This is not the result of inept trade policy administration but is a risk inherent in the political process.

Given U.S. experience with section 301, which chapter 2 notes is closely related to VIEs, there is justification for the fear that the United States will tacitly request or receive preferential market access. Such outcomes were seen when the unilateral U.S. attack on unfair foreign trade policies reached a peak in 1985–1989 with the active self-initiation of section 301 cases and the enactment of the super 301 amendment. Bhagwati (1988, 84) discusses how the United States rejected a Japanese proposal to replace its quota on leather and leather footwear with a tariff because that change might have reduced the U.S. share of the market. East Asian countries threatened by section 301 action during this period, such as Korea and Taiwan, responded by announcing shopping lists of U.S. goods they promised to buy. Korea announced a buying mission that intended to purchase $2.6 billion of U.S. goods in 1987. These purchases were often a pure trade diversion—taking a given volume of imports and allocating them to a different country—rather than trade creation. To placate the United States, Korea boasted that "the Procurement Office of the Korean Government signed a contract to purchase 20 dump trucks . . . from Caterpillar, even though the price of Averning Co. of the U.K. was about $100,000 lower than that of Caterpillar."[8] So blatant were these Buy American policies that Japan complained before the GATT about the preferential treatment that Korea afforded the United States.

Section 301 actions have also led to the sharing of rents in a foreign market rather than opening markets on principle. In a 1986 agreement ending a section 301 dispute concerning restrictions in the Korean insurance market, two U.S. firms already in that market received permission to participate in the lucrative, compulsory fire pool and one U.S. firm was licensed to enter the life insurance market. As Cho Yoon-Je (1987, 493) described it, "In the negotiations both governments, and especially the United States, basically represented the interests of their insurance industries . . . both governments approached the case with the perception that the main issue was the

8. Hyundai Heavy Industries "transfer[ed] considerable purchases from Japan to the U.S." by importing $3 million of welding bars. Korea also shifted $400 million in sales from Japan to United States and aimed to satisfy virtually all its agricultural grain imports from the United States (Republic of Korea 1987, 23).

sharing of profits in Korea's insurance markets."[9] The semiconductor case may reflect the same behavior.

Genuine liberalization of government trade restraints can result in an open, competitive market with free trade as the outcome. Imposing VIEs, particularly where the complaint rests on unspecified discrimination or different market structures or informal sales barriers, risks degenerating into discriminatory and preferential treatment for certain suppliers. This leads straight to trade diversion and constitutes export protectionism for one's own producers.

VIEs Exacerbate the Political Capture of U.S. Trade Policy

Just as domestic import-competing interests lobby for VERs, domestic exporting interests—given the opportunity—will lobby for VIEs. A general policy of seeking VIEs widens the door for private business interests to capture U.S. trade policy and reduces the government to an agent for these interest groups. For many years, U.S. semiconductor policy was driven by

---

9. With Japan's insurance market, the United States may oppose deregulation if that harms the position of the few U.S. firms in the market. Deputy U.S. Trade Representative Charlene Barshefsky recently testified, "As we look at economic reform and deregulation, we have to be absolutely vigilant to be sure that those reforms don't further disadvantage foreign competition." Apparently, the United States would oppose domestic reforms in the Japanese economy if they harm the position of U.S. firms in the market. See the *International Trade Reporter,* October 13, 1993.

an industry association dominated by one segment of the industry, a handful of relatively small merchant firms. During the negotiation of the 1986 U.S.-Japan semiconductor agreement, SIA representatives were often in the next room and received frequent updates from U.S. negotiators about the status of the talks; those negotiators also solicited the industry's views on an agreeable negotiating posture. Indeed, the SIA had veto power over any U.S.-Japan agreement. After the 1991 renegotiation of the agreement, Deputy U.S. Trade Representative S. Linn Williams was asked how the final accord differed from what the SIA (albeit this time in conjunction with downstream semiconductor users) had envisioned, he replied, "I would characterize most of these differences as questions of technical matters, not policy."[10] Sectoral trade policies often reflect merely the position of the most politically astute industry interest groups.

As Bergsten and Noland (1993, 191) note, the United States "has a producer-oriented, complainant-initiated trade policy system." The problem facing U.S. trade policy agencies—except for the Department of Commerce, which in most instances simply sides with the complainant—is to screen legitimate from illegitimate complaints. This raises the question of what criteria are used in picking and choosing the industries to benefit from U.S. government action. This is the classic economic problem of adverse selection: how to verify whether an intangible foreign trade barrier actually exists and whether the U.S. industry is truly competitive, or whether that industry is simply looking to capture a share of a lucrative

---

10. Press statement, June 4, 1991, quoted in Irwin (1994).

71

foreign market that it cannot achieve through competition over price and quality.

The arbitrary nature of selecting industries for VIEs raises the possibility that political pressures result in the wrong sectors chosen for a VIE. This could actually reduce the economic welfare of the United States if there is an expansion in output from a sector of the U.S. economy that benefits from government subsidies or price supports. Section 301 actions to open the tobacco market in Japan, Korea, Taiwan, and Thailand promised the expansion of U.S. output in a subsidized sector of the economy. In 1986 and 1988, the Rice Millers' Association filed section 301 petitions against Japan's barriers against foreign rice. Although both petitions were rejected on foreign policy grounds (because rice is a tremendously sensitive issue in domestic Japanese politics), this particular political rationale for inaction is not always present. Because U.S. rice production is directly and indirectly subsidized, an increase in exports does not correspond with an increase in U.S. economic welfare: expansion of output in a price-distorted sector of the U.S. economy might only magnify the distortion and detract from U.S. economic welfare.[11]

That the Clinton administration is no different from its predecessors in its ability to contain the private capture of public policy is illustrated in a virtual repeat of the semiconductor trade dispute in

---

11. According to the Congressional Budget Office, U.S. rice producers received more than $600 million in direct cash (deficiency) payments and net loan disbursements in the early 1990s. This figure does not include other indirect subsidies, such as the below-market prices for water use enjoyed by rice farmers in California.

1992–1993 with South Korea as the defendant. In this instance, the administration's embrace of import targets stumbled on the political realities of trade policy determination. In April 1992, Micron Technology, Inc., a small semiconductor producer in Boise, Idaho, filed an antidumping petition alleging less-than-fair-value imports of 1M DRAM semiconductors and higher from Korea. In October, the Commerce Department announced preliminary dumping margins (based on petitioner information) as high as 87 percent against Samsung, Goldstar, and Hyundai.

Faced with stiff antidumping duties, the Korean industry and government proposed in January 1993 a bilateral semiconductor trade agreement fashioned on the earlier one with Japan. In exchange for a suspension of the antidumping case, the Korean industry promised to monitor prices of export sales to the United States. The Korean government offered to sign an agreement committing itself to a VIE—or, as a draft stated, to "demonstrable and measurable results in terms of increasing sales in Korea of U.S. semiconductors and semiconductor equipment." The government also promised to reduce or to eliminate the Korean tariff on semiconductors, to secure greater intellectual property protection of U.S. chip designs, and to increase U.S. sales through other means.

Here, on its doorstep, was the prototype of a "market-opening" import target agreement that Clinton administration officials said they coveted, with another country that U.S. firms had complained about access—yet it was rejected. Confident of resting securely behind high antidumping duties imposed against Korea and itself unaffected by the prospective Korean market-opening actions, Micron vetoed the

Korean proposal. The USTR remained inert and basically ignored the Korean overture, and the Commerce Department represented its customer-client firm rather than act on a unique opportunity to improve access for all U.S. semiconductor firms in many desirable ways without necessarily setting import targets.[12]

In the end, in the Korea case just as in the Japan case, U.S. trade policy simply mirrored the concerns of the most vocal complainants—U.S. merchant firms—with little consideration of the nation's economic interest. VIEs will exacerbate this trend and will encourage even greater lobbying for export protectionism since the industries and sectors selected for VIEs are made in the political realm.

---

12. See *Inside U.S. Trade,* March 19, 1993.

SIX

Conclusions

The main goal of VIE proponents—reducing trade barriers in Japan—is certainly not at issue. Official government barriers to trade (not differences in market structure) are a legitimate target of U.S. trade policy and should be addressed within the present context of bilateral negotiations and the GATT system. When no government policies acting as trade barriers can be identified, however, resorting to managed trade arrangements in the form of VIEs is likely to be harmful.

This harm arises because, while conceptually different, VIEs are analytically similar to VERs. While VIEs are ostensibly designed to offset supposed trade restrictions rather than to create new ones, both are aspects of managed trade that entail the government's fixing market shares in international trade. Both tend to diminish competition by getting Japanese firms to reduce their sales, either in home or in foreign markets. Both are discriminatory and raise important third-party effects. Both are geared toward helping a select set of politically powerful domestic business

75

interests and risk being captured by these interests to the detriment of the broader domestic and international community's stake in an open world trading system. Both strengthen the role of MITI in influencing Japan's international trade patterns. But, in the end, Japan's economy cannot be truly liberalized by relying on the Japanese government to enforce import targets that attempt to mimic market outcomes.[1]

Skepticism of VIEs does not imply that Japan should be let off the hook in cases of demonstrably unfair government trade practices. Japan must now live up to the responsibility of upholding a liberal postwar international economic framework. In cases where clear government interferences exist—not complaints about low sectoral market shares or about differences in Japan's market structure—U.S. trade policy should address these problems.

But the intense obsession with Japan distorts the nature and depth of the problem of U.S. trade relations with Japan. Active use of VIEs in U.S. trade policy would reinforce the grossly exaggerated notion that foreign unfair trade practices excluding U.S. exports are a prominent feature of the international trading environment. A generous estimate of the increase in U.S. exports that would arise with a full liberalization of Japan's trade barriers, from Bergsten and Noland (1993, 189), is about $13.6 billion.[2] To

---

1. The new reformist government in Japan has recognized this and has therefore opposed VIEs. For an analysis along these lines, see Bhagwati (1994).

2. The comparison that is never made is the increase in U.S. imports from Japan that would result from the elimination of U.S. trade barriers against Japan, such as antidumping actions and voluntary restraint agreements.

put this figure in perspective, this is roughly a quarter of the U.S. bilateral trade deficit with Japan, 2 percent of U.S. exports of goods and services, and 0.2 percent of U.S. GDP in 1992. While this is not a trivial sum, it is much less than the emotive energy devoted to it. The completion of the Uruguay Round of trade negotiations under the GATT, for example, is reckoned to increase world income by more than $200 billion a year and to increase U.S. income by about $20 billion annually, but these figures do not receive the public attention that trade disputes with Japan do.[3]

Instead, the intense focus on Japan's hidden practices attracts undue attention to the vaporous idea of "international competitiveness" that Paul Krugman (1994) has so effectively demolished. It reinforces faulty notions about the nature and purpose of international trade and sustains the notion that Japan can be blamed for the economic shortcomings of the United States. The conviction that the United States is more open than other countries is perceived by U.S. policy makers as giving them the right to make unilateral demands on the trade policies of other countries.[4] U.S. trade policy is again

---

3. See Ian Goldin, Odin Knudsen, and Dominique van der Mensbrugghe (1993). These are real income gains, rather than the direct export sales figures calculated by Bergsten and Noland (which are higher than the actual real income gains).

4. In a great but common non sequitur, one U.S. trade official declared, as reported in the *Washington Post* of December 6, 1993: "We have the biggest trade deficit in the world. How can anybody call that a closed market?" For a recent discussion of U.S. trade barriers, see Gary C. Hufbauer and Kimberly Ann Elliott (1994).

taking on the tenor of a statement made in the mid-1980s by Senator Joseph Biden regarding international trade: "I don't want to compete, I just want to win." If this means fixing the results in foreign markets by setting market shares, so be it.

Blaming unfair discrimination abroad or unfair foreign business practices for our economic shortcomings is an easy way of avoiding serious discussion of domestic solutions. If the objective of the U.S. government is to reduce the current account deficit, reduction of the fiscal deficit and the promotion of domestic savings are a vastly superior approach to second-guessing market outcomes—or trying to mimic free market outcomes—by setting import targets for individual products in individual countries.

The United States can do much with its broad economic policies, such as fiscal policy and taxation, to encourage higher savings rates and greater accumulation of physical and human capital. These domestic issues should be the priorities for U.S. economic policy. Once our house is in order, the political pressures for the management of international trade will subside. Then, what should be the thrust of U.S. international trade policy—moving beyond the recently completed Uruguay Round to other areas for multilateral negotiation and strengthening the GATT's dispute settlement mechanism by taking cases there and adhering to their findings against the United States—can be accomplished in a less disputatious international environment.

VIEs, by contrast, are managed trade in the worst sense of the word. They do not make economic sense, they detract from the goal of liberalizing the Japanese economy, and they undermine the objective of an open, nondiscriminatory world trading system.

Analytical Notes on Voluntary Import Expansions

The debate over VIEs hinges crucially on whether setting import market share targets in the face of foreign trade barriers increases competition and moves firms toward free trade or reduces competition and fosters collusion. To address this issue, consider the simplest textbook model of oligopoly—the Cournot duopoly framework—which will serve as a stylized vehicle for examining the impact of VIEs on competition.[1]

Suppose two identical firms, one Japanese and

---

1. While Elias Dinopoulos and Mordechai E. Kreinin (1990) usefully explore the impact of VIEs under perfect competition, this rules out the strategic interactions between firms that are key to the current debate. This section was written before Theresa M. Greaney (1993) and Neil Bjorksten (1994) were available; those undertake a more formal analysis of the issue addressed here.

FIGURE A–1
Duopoly Equilibrium with a Voluntary Import Expansion

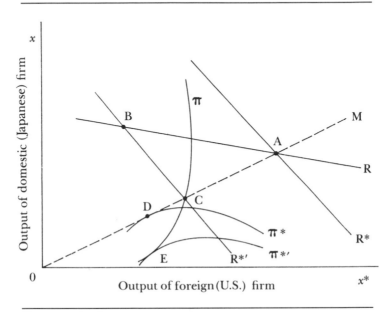

SOURCE: Author.

the other American, sell a homogeneous product either as a final good to Japanese households or an intermediate good to other Japanese firms. Further suppose that they produce this good under constant costs and compete in Japan in Cournot fashion; that is, each firm chooses its output to maximize profits, taking as given the output of its rival. Profit maximization implicitly defines a reaction function for each firm that renders its optimal (that is, profit-maximizing) output, given the output of the other firm. These are depicted in figure A–1, where x represents output

80

of the domestic (Japanese) firm and x^* represents output of the foreign (U.S.) firm. The Cournot-Nash equilibrium under free trade is at point A, where the two reaction functions (R for the Japanese firm, R^* for the U.S. firm) intersect.

Now assume that, for some unspecified reason, the Japanese market is difficult to penetrate. Discriminatory barriers or preferences for Japanese goods are analytically equivalent to a Japanese tariff on U.S. goods; that is, there is an implicit tax on or discrimination against U.S. products. This shifts the U.S. reaction function back (with slope unchanged) to $R^{*\prime}$, and the new equilibrium with Japanese trade barriers is now B. At B, Japanese output is higher, U.S. output is lower, and the higher domestic price (stability conditions ensure that U.S. output falls more than Japanese output rises) makes Japanese consumers worse off. The international distribution of the firms' profits is also different at B—U.S. profits are lower, Japanese profits are higher. This generates complaints by U.S. firms that they cannot sell adequately in Japan, and the USTR sets out to negotiate a solution.

Suppose further that the hidden tax on U.S. products cannot be removed by negotiations.[2] Instead, USTR and MITI settle on a VIE such that the U.S. firm is guaranteed the same market share in Japan that would exist under free trade. This market share defines the ray OM, passing from the origin

---

2. If the implicit tax were the result of explicit government policies, such as customs procedures, certification requirements, or procurement practices, a negotiated reduction of the barrier would simply shift $R^{*\prime}$ back toward R^*.

through the free trade equilibrium A. Along this line, the market share of the U.S. firm is exactly that under free trade; to the right of the line, the U.S. firm's market share is higher; to the left, its share is lower. How does a binding VIE alter competition in this market? The new equilibrium depends crucially on the credibility of the enforcement mechanism by which MITI ensures that the market share target is met. Put differently, the equilibrium depends on which firm remains passive and which takes up a Stackelberg leadership position against the other. Two plausible stories can be told, but they arrive at similar results.[3]

First, assume that the U.S. firm does not change its behavior (its reaction function remains $R^{*\prime}$), putting the burden on the Japanese firm to ensure that the VIE is met—but also allowing it to maximize its profits along $R^{*\prime}$. In this case, the equilibrium will be a point C, where $R^{*\prime}$ and OM intersect. At C, the profits of the Japanese firm can be represented by the isoprofit contour π, which represents its highest possible profits along $R^{*\prime}$ while meeting the OM constraint. The VIE has shifted the distribution of profits away from the Japanese firm and back toward the U.S. firm; in fact, profits of both firms may be higher at C than at A, depending on how restrictive the implicit tax on the U.S. firm is. Although the market shares of the two firms replicate that under free trade, the output of both firms is much lower than under free trade.

---

3. A more formal analysis of VIEs in duopoly would focus on how the firms' strategies change in a simultaneous move game with the introduction of a VIE. See Kala Krishna (1989) for this approach with VERs.

Now consider a second case, in which the U.S. firm acts as a Stackelberg leader. Under this scenario, the U.S. firm realizes that its Japanese counterpart must adjust its output to satisfy the VIE. The U.S. firm can therefore commit to an output level that maximizes its profits along the Japanese firm's reaction function, which has become the kinked line OAR. The U.S. firm's Stackelberg position is at point D, where its isoprofit contour π^* is tangent to OAR. This raises the possibility (not shown in figure A–1) that U.S. sales are lower under the VIE (at D) than under the implicit tax (at B).[4] Once again, the VIE shifts profits away from the Japanese firm and toward the U.S. firm, with the possibility that both firms' profits are higher at D than at A. Once again, output is much lower than under free trade even though the market shares of the two firms replicate what would exist under free trade.

The VIE is not voluntary for the Japanese firm. While its profits are higher with the VIE (at either C or D) than under free trade (at A), the firm would prefer the status quo (hidden barriers) and its high profits at point B. To induce the Japanese firm to sacrifice its profits voluntarily, MITI must threaten the firm with even larger sanctions if the VIE is not met. The credibility of these sanctions crucially affects whether the final equilibrium is at C or D. If the VIE is fully credible—the Japanese firm will absolutely ensure that the market share target will be met—then the U.S. firm can play off this certainty and become the Stackelberg leader, leading to equi-

---

4. U.S. output will also be lower when the U.S. firm is the Stackelberg leader compared with its output when the Japanese firm is the leader.

librium *D*. If, however, uncertainty exists about whether MITI has the power (administrative guidance, moral suasion, or whatever tools at its disposal) to compel the reluctant Japanese firm to comply with the VIE, then this uncertainty compels the U.S. firm to sell as usual (that is, to remain passive along $R^{*'}$), and the equilibrium will be at *C*. (We assume here that the VIE is binding ex post and ignore the case in which the Japanese firm chooses not to comply.)

Regardless of which scenario is more plausible, VIEs clearly neither enhance competition nor move the market toward a free trade equilibrium in this standard framework. Instead, VIEs prove to be much like a facilitating practice: market share targets fundamentally change the way firms interact in the market and bring about a more collusive outcome.[5] Such a conclusion is not surprising: A. Michael Spence (1978) has shown that a duopoly with market share strategies also leads to a collusive equilibrium.

Another possible outcome is that, on the announcement of a VIE, both firms recognize that cooperation to maximize joint profits—that is, cartel formation—is the best way to satisfy the import target and to reduce trade tensions.[6] A collusive equilibrium would

5. Krishna (1989) coined the phrase "facilitating practice" in her analysis of how a VER set at a free trade level brings about an outcome like collusion and increases the profits of both firms.

6. This begs the question of why the firms did not collude to increase profits in the first place. Presumably, one of the governments would have looked askance at such a practice before the trade dispute. The VIE provides the necessary cover against antitrust concerns; both governments are likely to be relieved that their firms are cooperating to diminish the trade conflict.

take place somewhere along the set of points in which the isoprofit contours of each firm are tangent to one another (the contract curve). Such an equilibrium is illustrated, for example, by point E, where $\pi^{*\prime}$ is tangent to π. (At this point, U.S. profits are higher than at point C, but Japan's profits are unchanged.) In this case, VIEs are the import counterpart to VERs and similarly tend to promote collusion.[7]

This simple example highlights an important political economy danger of VIEs. The import expansion failed to increase competition in Japan and merely shifted profits toward the U.S. firm. Should the United States strive for VIE agreements as a regular practice, the door opens to the rent-seeking activities of private U.S. firms willing to invest resources into the political market to capture a profit-shifting VIE for its own benefit, regardless of whether the policy has an underlying economic efficiency rationale.

There is yet another political economy reason for wariness toward VIEs. Suppose the Japanese government actually can open the market and establish the free trade equilibrium A by eliminating the implicit tariff that restricts the U.S. reaction function to $R^{*\prime}$. The Japanese firm will recognize that this will reduce its profits and will pressure the government to opt for

---

7. Proponents are likely to be unimpressed by this implication and may invoke some unspecified, "dynamic" procompetitive effects of VIEs. As Tyson (1990, 181) puts it: "From a static perspective, the [import] target may look like nothing more than a buyer's cartel or a tax on the importing country. But from a dynamic perspective, the target sets in motion changes in supply and demand behavior that can increase competition in both the importing country and the world market."

a VIE, allowing the firm to maintain higher profits at
C, D, or E rather than at A. Thus, even if free trade is a
viable option, firms in both countries will lobby for a
VIE to serve as a facilitating practice to mask their collusion.

References

Advisory Committee for Trade Policy and Negotiations. "Major Findings and Policy Recommendations on U.S.-Japan Trade Policy." Washington, D.C., January 1993.

Bambrick, Richard. "As Japan Clout Grows, Loyalty to U.S. Semiconductor Firms Tested." *Electronic News*, December 9, 1985, p. S28.

Bergsten, C. Fred. "Good and Bad of Managed Trade." *Financial Times*, August 18, 1993, p. 10.

Bergsten, C. Fred, and William R. Cline. *The United States-Japan Economic Problem*, 2d ed. Washington, D.C.: Institute for International Economics, 1987.

Bergsten, C. Fred, and Marcus Noland. *Reconcilable Differences? United States–Japan Economic Conflict.* Washington, D.C.: Institute for International Economics, June 1993.

Bhagwati, Jagdish. "VERs, Quid Pro Quo DFI, and VIEs: Political-Economy Theoretic Analyses." *International Economic Journal* 1 (Spring 1987): 1–14. Reprinted in Douglas A. Irwin, ed. *Political Economy and International Economics.* Cambridge: MIT Press, 1991.

———. *Protectionism.* Cambridge: MIT Press, 1988.

———. *The World Trading System at Risk.* Princeton: Princeton University Press, 1991.

———. "Samurais No More." *Foreign Affairs* 73 (May/June 1994): 2–7.

87

Bhagwati, Jagdish, and Douglas Irwin. "The Return of the Reciprocitarians: U.S. Trade Policy Today." *World Economy* 10 (June 1987): 109–30.

Bhagwati, Jagdish, and Hugh T. Patrick, eds. *Aggressive Unilateralism*. Ann Arbor: University of Michigan Press, 1990.

Bjorksten, Neil. "Voluntary Import Expansions and Voluntary Export Restraints in an Oligopoly Model with Capacity Constraints." *Canadian Journal of Economics* 27 (May 1994): 446–57.

Council on Competitiveness. *Roadmap for Results: Trade Policy, Technology and American Competitiveness.* Washington, D.C.: CoC, July 1993.

Dinopoulos, Elias, and Mordechai E. Kreinin. "Effects of the U.S.-Japan Auto VER on European Prices and on U.S. Welfare." *Review of Economics and Statistics* 70 (August 1988): 484–91.

Dinopoulos, Elias, and Mordechai Kreinin. "An Analysis of Import Expansion Policies." *Economic Inquiry* 28 (January 1990): 99–108.

Dixit, Avinash, "Comment on Tyson." In Robert Z. Lawrence and Charles L. Schultze, eds. *An American Trade Strategy: Options for the 1900s.* Washington, D.C.: Brookings Institution, 1990.

Dornbusch, Rudiger W. "Policy Options for Freer Trade: The Case for Bilateralism." In Robert Z. Lawrence and Charles L. Schultze, eds. *An American Trade Strategy: Options for the 1990s.* Washington, D.C.: Brookings Institution, 1990.

Finger, J. Michael. "Effects of the Kennedy Round Tariff Concessions on the Exports of Developing Countries." *Economic Journal* 86 (March 1976): 87–95.

Finger, J. Michael, and K. C. Fung. "Can Competition Policy Control 301?" Policy Research Working Paper 1253, World Bank, February 1994.

Flamm, Kenneth. "Semiconductor Dependency and Strategic Trade Policy." *Brookings Papers on Economic Activity,* Microeconomics 1:1993, pp. 249–325.

Gold, Peter L., and Dick K. Nanto. "Japan-U.S. Trade: U.S. Exports of Negotiated Products, 1985–1990." Congressional Research Service Paper 91–891E, December 1991.

Goldin, Ian, Odin Knudsen, and Dominique van der Mensbrugghe. *Trade Liberalization: Global Economic Implications.* Paris: Organization for Economic Co-operation and Development and World Bank, 1993.

Greaney, Theresa M. "Import Now! An Analysis of Voluntary Import Expansions (VIEs) to Increase U.S. Market Shares in Japan." Unpublished paper, University of Michigan, December 1993.

Hamilton, David P., and Bob Davis. "Chip Makers Call for Easing Burden on Japan." *Wall Street Journal,* June 7, 1993.

Hufbauer, Gary C., and Kimberly Ann Elliott. *The Costs of U.S. Trade Barriers.* Washington, D.C.: Institute for International Economics, 1994.

Irwin, Douglas A. "Trade Politics and the Semiconductor Industry." Paper prepared for the NBER Conference on the Political Economy of Protection, February 1994.

Ito, Takatoshi. *The Japanese Economy.* Cambridge: MIT Press, 1992.

Johnson, Chalmers. "*Keiretsu:* An Outsider's View." *International Economic Insights,* September/October 1990, pp. 15–17.

Kissinger, Henry, and Cyrus Vance. "Bipartisan Objectives for American Foreign Policy." *Foreign Affairs* 66 (Summer 1988): 899–921.

Krishna, Kala. "Trade Restrictions as Facilitating

Practices." *Journal of International Economics* 26 (May 1989): 251–70.

Krugman, Paul. "Competitiveness: A Dangerous Obsession." *Foreign Affairs* 73 (March/April 1994): 28–44.

Lake, David. *Power, Protection, and Free Trade: International Sources of U.S. Commercial Strategy, 1887–1939.* Ithaca: Cornell University Press, 1988.

Lawrence, Robert Z. "Efficient or Exclusionist? The Import Behavior of Japanese Corporate Groups." *Brookings Papers on Economic Activity* 1991:1, pp. 311–41.

Lineback, Robert J. "Sparks Fly, Briefly, over Europe-Japan Trade." *Electronic News,* December 14, 1992, p. 23.

National Research Council. *U.S.-Japan Strategic Alliances in the Semiconductor Industry.* Washington, D.C.: National Academy Press, 1992.

Pollack, Andrew. "U.S. Asks Favoritism in Cars despite Accord with Japan." *New York Times,* October 28, 1993.

Reid, T. R. "Trade Talks Turn Aggressive." *Washington Post,* December 6, 1993.

Republic of Korea, Embassy. "Market-Opening, Tariff Reductions and Other Trade Liberalization Measures Taken by the Korean Government in 1987," June 1987.

Saxonhouse, Gary. "What Does Japanese Trade Structure Tell Us about Japanese Trade Policy?" *Journal of Economic Perspectives* 7 (Summer 1993): 21–43.

Semiconductor Industry Association. *Four Years of Experience under the U.S.-Japan Semiconductor Agreement: "A Deal Is a Deal."* November 1990.

Semiconductor Industry Association and Dewey Ballantine. *Japanese Market Barriers in Microelectronics.* Memorandum in Support of a Petition Pursuant to

Section 301 of the Trade Act of 1974, as amended, June 14, 1985.

Sheard, Paul. "*Keiretsu* and Closeness of the Japanese Market: An Economic Appraisal." Institute of Social and Economic Research Discussion Paper 273, Osaka University, June 1992.

Spence, A. Michael. "Efficient Collusion and Reaction Functions." *Canadian Journal of Economics* 11 (August 1978): 527–33.

Tyson, Laura D'Andrea. "Managed Trade: Making the Best of the Second Best." In Robert Z. Lawrence and Charles L. Schultze, eds. *An American Trade Strategy: Options for the 1990s.* Washington, D.C.: Brookings Institution, 1990.

———. *Who's Bashing Whom? Trade Conflict in High-Technology Industries.* Washington, D.C.: Institute for International Economics, 1992.

United States. *Economic Report of the President.* February 1994.

———. Global Partnership Plan of Actions. January 1992.

———. Arrangement between the Government of Japan and the Government of the United States of America Concerning Trade in Semiconductor Products. June 11, 1991.

United States, Office of the U.S. Trade Representative. *Report on Foreign Trade Barriers.* 1993.

Weinstein, David E., and Yishay Yafeh. "Japan's Corporate Groups: Collusive or Competitive? An Empirical Investigation of *Keiretsu* Behavior." Harvard Institute of Economic Research Discussion Paper 1623, January 1993.

Yaginuma, Hisashi. "The *Keiretsu* Issue: A Theoretical Approach." *Japanese Economic Studies,* Spring 1993, pp. 3–48.

Yoon-Je, Cho. "How the United States Broke into Korea's Insurance Market." *World Economy* 10 (December 1987): 483–96.

About the Author

DOUGLAS A. IRWIN is an associate professor of business economics in the Graduate School of Business of the University of Chicago. He has previously served on the staff of the Council of Economic Advisers (1986–1987) and in the International Finance Division of the Federal Reserve Board (1988–1991).

A NOTE ON THE BOOK

*This book was edited by Ann Petty of the
publications staff of the American Enterprise Institute.
The text was set in Baskerville.
Coghill Composition Company of Richmond, Virginia,
set the type, and Data Reproductions Corporation
of Rochester Hills, Michigan, printed and bound the book,
using permanent acid-free paper.*

The AEI Press is the publisher for the American Enterprise Institute for Public Policy Research, 1150 17th Street,
N.W., Washington, D.C. 20036; *Christopher C. DeMuth,*
publisher; *Dana Lane,* director; *Ann Petty,* editor; *Cheryl
Weissman,* editor; *Lisa Roman,* editorial assistant (rights and
permissions).

DATE DUE